What Helps: Sixty Slogans to Live By
Satya Robyn

Previous books by Satya Robyn

Just As You Are: Buddhism for Foolish Beings
(with Kaspalita Thompson)

Thaw

Small Kindnesses

The Letters

The Most Beautiful Thing

Afterwards

Some Kind of Freak

What Helps
Sixty Slogans to Live By

Satya Robyn

Woodsmoke Press

What Helps: Sixty Slogans to Live By
ISBN: 978-0-9931317-4-5

Published by Woodsmoke Press 2018
Copyright © 2018 Satya Robyn

Satya Robyn asserts the moral right to be identified as the author of this work.
All rights reserved.

Cover design by Kaspalita Thompson

Woodsmoke Press
Amida Mandala Buddhist Temple
Malvern
WR14 4AA

kaspa@woodsmokepress.com
www.woodsmokepress.com

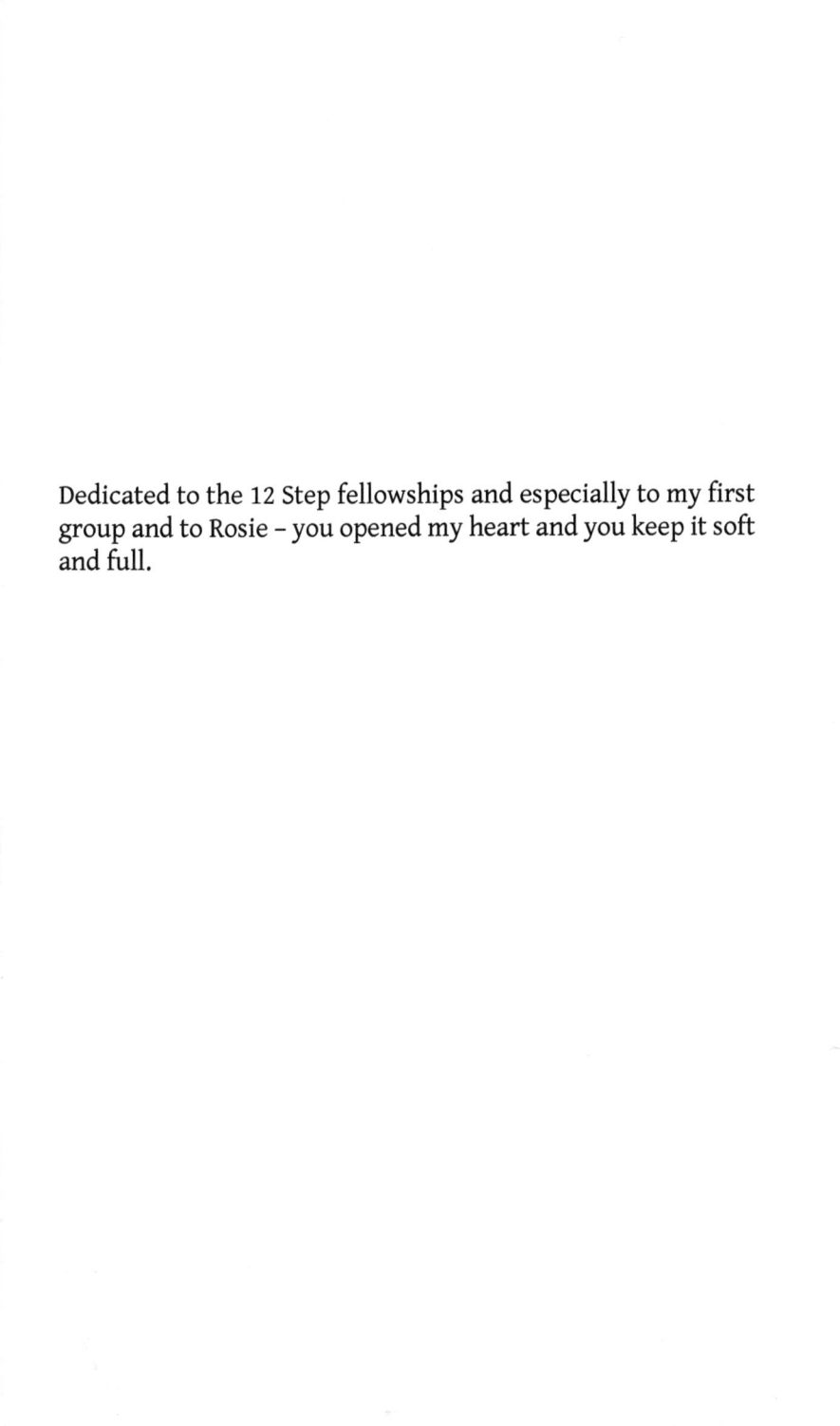

Dedicated to the 12 Step fellowships and especially to my first group and to Rosie – you opened my heart and you keep it soft and full.

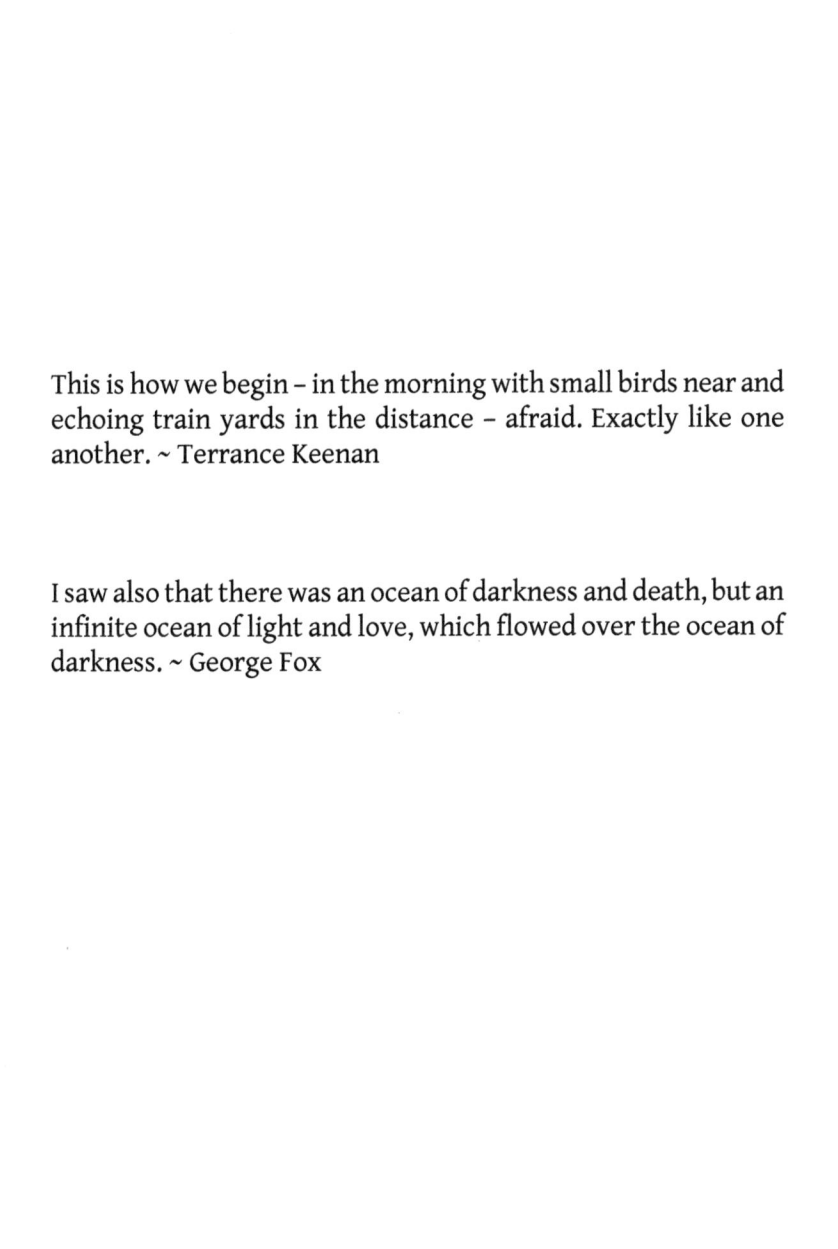

This is how we begin – in the morning with small birds near and echoing train yards in the distance – afraid. Exactly like one another. ~ Terrance Keenan

I saw also that there was an ocean of darkness and death, but an infinite ocean of light and love, which flowed over the ocean of darkness. ~ George Fox

Contents

Introduction	1
Your koan	3
How to make friends with this book	6
Begin here	8
Be bombu	11
Let the light in	16
Rest	19
Wake up	24
Worst things first	29
Listen to your body	33
Eat art	36
Do something small	40
Embrace dependency	46
Find fellow feeling	51
Surrender control	54
Grow gratitude	59
Hand it over	63
Structures support us	67
Make space to create	71
Everything changes	75
Hold on	79
Keep walking	83

Nature heals	86
Know yourself	89
Peaks and troughs	95
Detach with love	99
Bow often	105
Ask for help	110
Chuck should	118
Be heard	122
Change your conditions	128
Progress not perfection	135
Lean in	140
Attend to others	145
Seek sangha	149
Make offerings	153
Take refuge	157
Honour work	161
Make mistakes	166
Lighten up	171
Radical honesty	175
When you can't stop it, clock it	179
Let go of clinging	185
Savour solitude	190
Step towards fear	194
If in doubt, wait	198

Write things right	202
Make vows	208
Simplify	212
Find faith	216
Open your heart	222
Choose joy	225
Pray	229
Set boundaries	233
No blame	240
Be kind	247
Love everything	251
Remember death	255
Feel your feelings	261
Relax	268
Trust the process	272
Open to the Other	278
Just as you are	282
Postscript	285
The Right Medicine	287
Books that might help	289

Introduction

This book is a love letter.

I don't know you, but I can make a few guesses about you. You were born with a fallible human body, to two parents who did their best but occasionally (or often) got it spectacularly wrong. Each morning you wake up and face a day full of things-that-need-doing and responsibilities that pull you in different directions. You are in relationships that are variously disappointing, nourishing, agonising, inspiring, monotonous, wildly unpredictable, and all the rest. Sometimes you wonder what it's all for. You have a long list of fears, and some hope. You have a limited amount of life left.

This book is a love letter to you. Lorna Crozier says that "the books that readers cherish make them feel less alone." I want you to find solace here. I want you to feel hugged. I also want to extend some invitations, offer some insights, and introduce some new possibilities – possibilities which might take you into uncomfortable territory. I'll do this because I want to see your shoulders relaxing, your chin lifting, and your heart softening. I want to hear you laugh. I want to see you doing the things you really want to do. I want you to be kinder to others, and kinder to yourself. I want you to want to write love letters.

This book is also a love letter to myself. I have been learning, little by little, to look after myself over the past thirty years. I'm still a work-in-progress, as we all are, but I do it much better these days. This book is where I will remind myself of all the things I've learnt. We tend to have short memories when it comes to this kind of learning.

The title of this book came to me one morning as I was sitting in meditation in our shrine room. I live on the ground floor of the Buddhist temple I run with my husband, and so I have a very short commute to morning meditation. As I sat and let the busy work-thoughts subside, two words floated towards me through the waking-up fog – What Helps. They didn't have a question mark on the end. They were presented to me as an invitation.

Of course, I'm not the first one to have shared any of the wisdom in this book. I have been offered so many glittering wisdom-jewels; by people who've cared about me, through books, as a result of horrible situations, through nature and elsewhere. Some slipped through my fingers many times before I learnt how to grasp them. Some are still slipping through. The wonderful thing about these jewels is that they self-replicate, and when you give them away your own jewel shines even more strongly. In these pages I'll do my best to transmit the essence of all I've received so far. Hopefully you'll get to keep one or two beauties. Maybe they'll be smooth and lapis lazuli blue, or maybe they'll be the swirled iridescence of mother-of-pearl.

I have received so many gifts. Here they are. Please – take whatever is useful, and pass them on.

Your koan

Keep two pieces of paper in your pockets at all times. One that says 'I am a speck of dust.' And the other, 'The world was created for me.'
~ Rabbi Bunim of P'shiskha

What koans are you bringing to this book?

Koan (pronounced ko-ahn) is a Japanese word describing a form of Zen Buddhist practice where the student is given a story or a question with an impossible answer or conclusion. In this practice you are told to contemplate the koan you are given (examples are 'Who is it who now repeats the Buddha's name?' or 'What is the sound of one hand clapping?') and then present your answer to your Buddhist teacher. It can take many years for a teacher to be satisfied with the student's response to their koan. Koans are intended to drive you a little crazy, and to help you to make contact with great doubt, great faith and ultimately enlightenment.

We can also use the word koan to refer to a particular tangle or question-without-answer that keeps coming up in our own life. One of my koans is how I struggle to find a middle path between the extremes of over-indulgence and deprivation, and this shows up in different areas of my life – how I eat (sometimes binging, sometimes being disciplined), how I work (compulsive overwork or falling into laziness) etc. Another of my current koans is how to hold onto my own process when I'm faced with someone's suffering or disapproval, rather than abandoning myself and leaping into attending to the other. Other personal koans might be 'when people really get to know me they won't want to stay around', 'what does it all mean', 'what do I want', struggles to commit or to be intimate in relationships, or a deep fear of impermanence.

These koans can often underlie the smaller knots that we encounter in our daily lives. I might find myself avoiding someone because they have disapproved of my work in the past. I might feel uncomfortable around illness because it points towards my huge fear of death. It's good to make sense of or untangle the little knots, and it's also good to keep the possibility of bigger patterns in mind, or we'll just keep making new tangles.

Before you read on, you might want to pause for a few minutes and list a few of your koans. Write them down somewhere, and return to them as you read on. You might find that you can articulate them more clearly as you continue to read. You might discover how your small daily dissatisfactions sit on top of one of them like ticks on a koan-sheep! This book will help you find some fresh new responses to them.

It might also help you to remember that koans aren't something that get in the way of our progress towards wisdom and happiness. They're not boulders on the path. Working on our koans *is* the path. I agree that it doesn't always feel that way, when we're bashing up against them, and when we're confused or frustrated or in pain. Just don't be too quick to give up on the process, or to judge whether the final results will be good or bad. Allow for the possibility that you are learning what you need to learn, in the only way you can learn it. To replace the metaphorical path with a river, allow the water to carry you forwards, and enjoy as much of the view as you can. I'll be floating along beside you.

How to make friends with this book

I know you're tired but come, this is the way.
~ Rumi

There are three ways you could approach this book.

The first is to start at the beginning and read it through to the end. Carry your koans with you and see what happens along the way.

The second is to look at the chapter headings and to dive straight into the chapters you feel most drawn to.

The third is to let Lady Luck show you the way – use the Right Medicine chapter at the end of the book.

There are questions at the end of each chapter. Answer them in your head or, if you want to squeeze out more juice, write the answers down in a beautiful notebook. If a related question comes to your mind, write that down and answer it too. Don't be afraid of having conversations with yourself, or between different parts of yourself. It's good to get the different bits talking.

The chapters are designed to be read more than once. I'd encourage you to read them slowly – like tasting expensive dark chocolate. You may find particular phrases that resonate – write them down. You may find it helpful to read particular chapters out loud.

Each chapter heading contains the meaning of the chapter in concentrated form. If there are chapters that you find particularly helpful, remember the chapter title as a slogan. Put some of these slogans in your pockets as if they are smooth pebbles from a sun-drenched day at the beach and carry them with you out into the world.

Are you ready for your first slogan?

Begin here

> *What can anyone give you greater than now, starting here, right in this room, when you turn around? ~ William Stafford*

The beginning is always here. Right now I am sitting on one of the grey bucket chairs in my office – the chair that faces the window. I'm looking out onto a strip of lawn and a bird feeder which is swaying in the cold November wind. The garden drops away steeply and above a low ivy-covered wall is a swathe of the Severn valley, today pale with mist. Bredon Hill is in the far distance, and between me and it there are houses and a church steeple and trees and fields. Later the town's street lights will start coming on one by one and will ornament the darkness with gold.

I heard some advice once about what to do when you receive very bad news, like the unexpected death of someone close to you. It was suggested that after finishing the terrible conversation you go and do exactly what it was you were about to do. Maybe you put the phone down and finish hanging out the laundry, or continue writing the email and send it off. I don't know how this works in practice as I haven't needed to try it out yet, but I imagine that it has the effect of stitching you back into the world, at a time when everything is threatening to dissolve or blow into pieces. Here – I can pick up this damp sock and hang it up. Here – I can shake the creases out of this pair of trousers. These are the things that I still know and can do and these are the things that need to be done. This is how life goes on.

Wherever we are and whatever is happening, we can always return to the material world. We can return to the objects around us, and to our bodies. We can bring our attention to the sparkling freshness of the here-and-now. Here. I've got one of my legs, my left one, tucked up underneath me. It's asking me to move it soon. In front of me is the low table covered with a gold cloth that sits between me and my psychotherapy clients. A dark grey stone Buddha sits on it, hands folded on his lap, lit up by a tea-light in a red lotus flower candle holder, the petals translucent. Now. In ten minutes I have a Skype session with a client in Canada, but right now I am tasting a gingerbread truffle and moving my cold fingers across the keyboard.

This is my beginning for this book. Here in my office with its Buddhas, its powder blue end walls, my books, the view, my cat-scratched rug, my damp red sock draped over the armrest of the chair. What is your beginning? What is your here-and-now?

The questions at the end of each chapter will give you an opportunity to become properly present. I don't want you to just swallow my words whole (or spit them straight out) – I'd like you to swish them around in your mouth for a while. I'd like you to stitch yourself into this book. Take as long as you like to find your own answers – I'll be here when you get back.

Questions for reflection

What can you see, smell, hear, feel and taste?

What is happening in your body right now?

What are you thinking?

What are you feeling?

What do you fear here and now?

What do you hope here and now?

What do you want here and now?

What do you need here and now?

What can you offer here and now?

Be bombu

> *I don't know what I'm doing most of the time. There's a certain humor in realizing that. I can never figure out the kind of tie to put on in the morning. I don't have any strategy or plan to get through the day. It is literally a problem for me to decide which side of the bed to get out on. These are staggering problems. I remember talking to this Trappist monk in a monastery. He's been there twelve years. A pretty severe regime. I expressed my admiration for him and he said 'Leonard, I've been here twelve years and every morning, I have to decide whether I'm going to stay or not.' I knew exactly what he was talking about.*
> ~ Leonard Cohen

Something that helps me a lot, and that I witness helping other people, is knowledge of what we Pureland Buddhists call the 'bombu paradigm'. This holds that we humans are all irrevocably bombu – a Japanese word that means 'foolish beings of wayward passions'.

The Buddha taught that we are all filled with greed, hate and delusion. As we encounter the world, we tend to have one of these three reactions – we like what happens and we want more, we don't like what happens and we don't want it to happen again, or we are confused or in denial about what happens. This grabbing, pushing away or ignoring all leads to us suffering, sooner or later.

As I sit here at my desk I am conscious of a sludgy feeling in my body from the cold I woke up with. As I write, I struggle to find the right word or the right way of saying what I want to say. My thoughts flick to the fact that I'm having a fast day today and not eating any lunch. I have an immediate negative reaction to all of these experiences. I try to push the hate away by staring out of the window when I can't think of the right word, or by fantasising about dinner in an attempt to comfort myself. The longer I avoid the writing, the worse I feel.

The small positive things that happen are more likely to result in greed. I glance over at the golden tongue-tip of the candle flame on my desk and enjoy watching it waver – I spend too long gazing at it and I neglect my work. Last night I enjoyed the taste of cake so much that I had another fat slice, one that left me feeling slightly sick. When we experience pleasure we tend to cling to it – rearranging the world in various ways so we can get more and then suffering the consequences.

Delusion is confusion, denial or 'not seeing clearly'. My Buddhist teacher Dharmavidya describes delusion as "...the distortion of perception and thinking brought about by the 'conceit of self' – attachment to the ideas we have of ourselves and particularly the tendency to regard oneself as a special case." This conceit prevents us from seeing the truth about a situation and so causes us to act in ways that are unhelpful. We can see delusion at play in small ways (we don't believe someone who compliments our cooking as we see ourselves as poor cooks) or much bigger ways (the denial that allows an alcoholic to continue drinking as their alcohol intake isn't as bad as their friends).

These drives or unwholesome mental states are also pretty insidious. We might think that we're doing something because it's a 'good thing to do', but when we look again we find that we're largely being driven by our selfish desires. We give to charity because we feel guilty about our relatively opulent lifestyle, or we offer to help a colleague because we want them to see us as a 'kind person'. We encourage a friend to talk because hearing about their crazy life makes ours look sane by comparison.

The bombu paradigm suggests that greed, hate and delusion are so deeply embedded in us, so overwhelming, that we are practically powerless to exert control over them. We are foolish beings of wayward passion. When we begin to see how consumed we are by our greed, hate and delusion it can feel a little depressing. We may internally rebel – we're not really so bad, are we? Surely this is an overly pessimistic way of seeing the world?

What helps us to be softer with ourselves and others is to remember why we are continually being triggered into greed, hate and delusion. We are scared. We are afraid of losing what we love and of having to endure what we don't want to endure. More fundamentally, underneath these simpler 'likes and dislikes' is a fear of impermanence, a fear of losing ourselves completely. If we see the truth of how changeable our personalities are over time, how can we continue to construct a coherent view of self? Who is Satya anyway? For the ego this is a life or death situation, and it takes action by constructing ever-more elaborate narratives or by attempting to manipulate the world. This is a doomed project as we will never find security in the midst of impermanence. No wonder we bob around so helplessly like corks on the wild seas of our passions.

When you resist the reality of your bombu nature, try to continue to be curious about yourself, keeping an open mind. Be gentle with your frightened ego. We are trying our best, but we are shoved around by our greed hate and delusion like the school bully. We attempt to re-write what's happened, creating flattering stories about ourselves, but we have acted foolishly, and we will do so again. As you begin to see yourself and your motivations more clearly, you may come to see how deeply we are deluded. No-one is exempt (unless they are a Buddha, and there aren't too many of those around) – we are all in the same boat.

Maintaining denial is tiring, and so truly seeing ourselves as hungry, frightened creatures releases us from a lot of hard work. I hope that when you approach this truth you will feel some of what I feel – a profound relief. We can acknowledge the vulnerable parts of ourselves and know that the light of compassion shines on them. We can also empathise with the bombu nature of others. This is how we are. And that is okay.

Questions for reflection

Are you bombu?

What are your especially bombu parts?

Are the people you know bombu?

When do you feel disappointed by their bombu nature?

When can you feel more empathetic towards them?

Can you think of an example of when you've retold a story so you came out as more of a hero, or slightly less of a fool?

Is it easier for you to identify with the greedy, hateful or deluded parts of yourself?

Where might you be in denial about your foolishness? What's your hunch? How might your loved ones answer this question?

When you imagine the depth of your foolishness, can you imagine it being seen by anyone or anything and accepted just as it is?

Can you acknowledge your bombu nature right now and trust that you are not alone?

Let the light in

> *The light will work its own good work*
> *If only we will trust it...*
> *~ from Tai Shi Chih's Prayer in the Nien Fo Book,*
> *the Prayer book of Amida Shu*

What is the light that works its own good work? Where does it come from? What work is it doing on us and on the world?

As I sit here at my desk and type, the light is the female blackbird who has just hopped into view on the muddy lawn outside my window. It is the breath that enters my body, and my shoulder muscles relaxing with tiny pops and crackles as I move my neck from side to side. It is the seeded toast and marmite I had for breakfast. It is the care I received from my mother when I was very young, and the way my husband took time out to listen to me carefully earlier this morning.

The light is anything that nourishes us. The light warms us, so we can begin to let go of unhealthy attachments. Sometimes this light can be fierce. A harsh word from a friend forces us to see a truth about ourselves that we've been fighting to avoid, or someone we care about dies and we feel propelled into booking the trip we've been meaning to take for years. Sometimes the light is so slow and gentle, it's practically invisible. We might set a firm intention to stop smoking five years before we're finally ready to do it, and the light is soaking into us all that time.

Some of us have favourite places to find the light. It might come to us when we go running or when we hang out with trees. We might connect with it when we read poetry, tinker with our motorbike or have good conversations with our friends.

The light always moves us in the direction of opening, relaxing and letting go. It slowly changes us into people who are more able to give, more able to enjoy our lives, and more able to love.

We block the light all the time. We think that we are keeping ourselves safe, or we simply don't recognise it for what it is. We are frightened to let go of the defences that have kept us safe for many years. We are afraid to be happy. We are afraid to be vulnerable, tender and open.

The light surrounds us. There are times when we can't see it, when it is hidden behind the clouds. Sometimes there are years when we only catch a glimpse. It doesn't abandon us, though – we abandon it, through our well-intentioned attempts to keep ourselves whole and sane. When we can't feel it, we can trust that it is there. When we can feel it, we can turn our faces like sunflowers and bathe in the light.

Questions for reflection

Can you feel any light in your body right now? Scan your body slowly and pause wherever you find any sensations that feel good or calm.

Can you see any light around you? Are there books in your room that bring you comfort, or memories that arise as you scan your surroundings?

How are you nourished by the light in your life right now?

Where are you blocking the light from entering you?

What long-term projects is the light working on inside you?

How can you carry the light with you as you read the rest of this book?

Rest

> *Build gaps in your life. Pauses. Proper pauses.*
> *~ Thom Yorke*

Resting is crucial. It allows us to empty ourselves out and become ready for whatever is next. It gives our bodies a chance to repair themselves, and our brains a chance to cool down after bouts of fizzing and popping. Rest is when the composting happens. Rest is the jar of silky mud and water shaken into a mud milkshake, which clears as the tiny particles take a slow shimmy to the bottom. Rest is the spaces between all the rest.

I resist rest. Knowing how to rest is a highly polished jewel that keeps on slipping through my fingers. Why can rest be so elusive? We might think we can blame the world for our relentless busy-ness. The world does pull at us with its insatiable demands – caring for children or parents, holding down our jobs, endless domestic tasks, juggling finances – but this isn't the whole picture.

I find that, at my worst, I resist rest so strongly that as I power through my 'list of things to do' I am simultaneously thinking up new items to add to the bottom of it. The faster I tick items off and the more desperate I am to 'get to the end of the list and rest', the more of them appear – just like baby rabbits. For me, not being able to rest isn't something that the world does to me. It's something that I, mostly unconsciously, do to myself.

My reasons for not resting include: deriving a sense of identity from being someone-who-achieves-lots-of-stuff, a fear of what might emerge from the silence of rest, an addiction to the buzzy nature of busy, an anxiety about not earning enough money, a guilt that arises when I stop working and more. There are layers and layers.

Despite all this creative self-sabotage, I have got better at resting. What has helped me, and what will help you?

Insert pauses. If you have five minutes to spare before you go somewhere or do something, don't squeeeeeeeze in one-more-thing-to-do. Instead sit and look at the sky, or shut your eyes, and notice your muscles letting go of themselves one by one. You might also like to breathe. If you are late, take thirty seconds before you rush off and do the same thing. There will always be one-more-thing-to-do. The things-to-do will never be done. The world will not stop turning if you leave some undone.

Schedule space. I need to block out longer rest periods into my diary to stop appointments multiplying and to protect some uncluttered white spaces. For me this rest space includes a Sabbath Day every Monday, and a proper retreat weekend every few months. I pay attention to what I'm doing during these times and try not to slide into working, seeing people who drain my energy or squeezing in too many leisure activities.

Creating a rest menu. On my menu are things like baking, napping, walking (but not up too many steep hills), drinking coffee in cafés, reading travel books and writing letters to my nieces. Activities that I'm tempted to include on my list but that actually leave me feeling less rested include compulsively surfing the internet, spending money on things I don't need and watching trashy television. Of course, there's a place for trashy television, but some rest activities can easily anaesthetize us and leave us with a muzzy head.

Tuning in to myself. When I take some time to tune in, I notice a squeezed feeling in my stomach when I become a bit manic. I recognise that my voice often goes croaky on a Friday, and this is because I am tired. I notice a feeling of overwhelm when I look at the things I've scheduled into my diary over the next few days. When I notice these things, I then have a choice about whether I change something or not. Sometimes this is a matter of scheduling in extra rest as soon as I can, and sometimes it means cancelling or rearranging things. Sometimes I need to lower my expectation of myself. Sometimes I need to go to bed and hide under the duvet without delay!

Giving myself permission. In the Tao Te Ching it says:

> *If you want to become full,*
> *let yourself be empty.*
> *If you want to be reborn,*
> *let yourself die.*

I don't feel that I should need to rest, ever. This message somehow imprinted itself into my bones, which means that I have to give myself permission to rest, over and over. I do this by reminding myself that rest is crucial if I want to become full again, if I want to be reborn, just like the fields that lie fallow. Even God rested on the seventh day.

Rest is delicious. It is a long drink of homemade lemonade on a hot day. It nourishes us and ultimately helps us to contribute more to the world and to those around us. Your body knows when you need rest. If you ignore it, it will shout louder and louder. Pay attention to its wisdom, make the changes you need to make, and lean back...

Questions for reflection

How good are you at resting?

What are your reasons for not resting?

What are the consequences of not getting enough rest for you? For those around you?

What feeds you when you rest? Walking? Cooking? Looking at the sky?

What could you add to your rest menu?

When can you schedule in some mini-spaces? Even six minutes with a cup of tea counts.

When can you schedule in some longer spaces?

Can you take a few minutes to rest right now? Maybe close your eyes, and feel your shoulders melting...

Wake up

> *Again and again I've taken quick glances and then for some reason I've got to sit before a picture waiting and it's opened up like one of those Japanese flowers that you put into water and something I thought wasn't worth more than a casual, respectful glance begins to open up depth after depth of meaning. ~ Sister Wendy Beckett*

Just to my right is a golden cat-sized Buddha sitting on the top of my bookcase. His eyes are just higher than my eyes, and he watches over me as I type. I gazed at him as I wondered where to start this chapter, and noticed that the pale blue silk he sits on has a silver filigree pattern of geometric flowers and leaves. It is beautiful, and it enriches my moment like salt in soup.

Paying attention is a choice that we can make at any moment. Most of us move through our days half-conscious, running on automatic, making a million assumptions a minute about our environment. We couldn't survive if we didn't have the ability to let parts of us sleep. Driving to work would be a trial if we were conscious of every movement of our hands on the steering wheel or the precise mechanics of each gear change. If we paid careful attention to the miniscule signs on the faces of people we interact with, noticing the subtle feelings that arise as we do, we would become exhausted.

Most of us, however, tend to drift towards the unconscious end of the scale. Who can blame us – life is complicated and difficult! But we are missing out on so much. The Zen master Ikkyu was once asked to write down a distillation of all his best teachings and he wrote only one word: 'Attention.' The visitor was disappointed, wanting more, and so Ikkyu wrote again: 'Attention. Attention.' If I hadn't taken a few extra seconds to gaze at the blue silk before I turned back to my computer, I wouldn't have discovered this faint pattern of silver tracings. I wouldn't have felt my heart swelling with beauty.

Waking up sometimes means noticing new super-fine details – how precisely does the air smell this morning? What exact colour and texture is the garden bench? Waking up sometimes means broadening our gaze. How is it to hear all the individual sounds of the forest as a symphony? What might be on the periphery of our vision, of our known experience?

Waking up brings us into a closer relationship with ourselves, with other people and with the world. This isn't always a comfortable experience. For a couple of months I walked past the cat shit which our old cat Fatty had kindly deposited all over our fallow vegetable patch. Whenever I saw it, the thought 'I should clear that up' was quickly followed by 'I don't want to face it right now'. I pushed the 'should' aside and nudged the resulting guilt into the dark recesses of my 'do it later' mind. When I finally got round to cleaning it up, it only took twenty minutes. I'd spent much longer avoiding it!

If I'd been able to feel the discomfort of seeing it more fully, I might have tackled it earlier. An intensification of feeling is one hallmark of being more awake. We might suddenly become more aware of the pain in our lower back, or an ache of sadness resting at the bottom of our throat. We might feel exhilaration as we look at clouds being shoved across the sky by strong winds. We notice things that we hadn't noticed before, both inside us and outside of us. We sometimes feel gratitude.

Unless we are enlightened already, we can't be awake all the time. Repression serves us – it gives us a place to put overwhelming emotion until we're ready to feel it. Our defences keep us safe. I like to see waking up as a vow or a direction I'm moving in, rather than something I expect to attain once and for all. It's not something that can be forced. We need to seduce ourselves into paying more attention, like drawing bunnies out of their hutch with a sweet carrot.

Something that will help you to wake up is writing a *small stone* every day. A *small stone* is a short piece of writing that captures a moment in time, just as a photograph might. The name is from the stones we pick up when we're on a long walk on the beach to carry home in our pockets. You don't have to be a writer to write *small stones*, you just have to pause once a day, open up your senses, and record what you experience. We can write *small stones* about the feathery tickle in our noses, the blobs of dew glistening on the hostas, a conversation we overhear, the smell of toast – anything that catches our attention and invites us to examine it more closely. Become conscious, tune in to what's inside and outside, and then enjoy playing with language, attempting to capture a little bubble of the world.

Don't underestimate the power of these few minutes where you stop and observe what's around you. Writing *small stones*, like anything that connects us to what is bigger than us, works like sliding a ruler into a small crack in our thick defences and gently levering them open. Even writing one a day snuggles us into the world and keeps our hearts and minds open.

Earlier in the week I was in the centre of a swirl of unhappiness and bad political news. Feeling unwell and ill at ease, I walked through the garden at dusk and wrote this series of *small stones* using the tools of careful observation followed by accurate description.

> *By the pond a brick sits, growing luxuriant lime-green moss. The magnolia is beginning to bud. Blackbird song slides towards me like strands of light. The sky is almost purple.*

> *The invisible badger has gouged new chunks from the lawn. I put the rabbits to bed, stroking the long soft hair on Poppet's neck. Safe in their hutch with hay and water and their warm nest.*

> *In the alcove, the gold seams of the Buddha's robes glint. Crisp leaves congregate around the skirts of his shrine-cloth. I go to him and lean my head in for a moment, resting it on his shoulder.*

Paying attention and recording small details grounds me and keeps me safe in difficult times. It helps me stay alive to whatever is true, as it shifts from moment to moment. It helps me to not turn my face away. It connects me into everything which, despite the cat shit and dispiriting politics, always connects me to gratitude.

Questions for reflection

How do you know when you are more awake? What happens in your body? What happens to your thoughts or feelings?

What helps you to wake up?

What do you pay attention to during your days?

Which of your senses do you enjoy? How could you indulge these senses?

Which senses do you tend to neglect?

Would you like to try writing a *small stone* every day for a week?

Could you spend a few minutes paying attention right now?

Worst things first

> *Our natural way of working is to follow the path of least resistance. If we are given a list of tasks, we will tend to do the easy ones first. The problem with this is that when we get to a certain level of difficulty, there is a tendency to invent more easy tasks to avoid having to do the more difficult tasks. That is one of the reasons people get submerged in a sea of trivia. If we reverse this and do the tasks we least want to first, then our day will get progressively easier and there will be no need to invent any more "busy work". ~ Mark Forster*

Just before I sat down to write this chapter, my husband Kaspa asked me if I wanted to join him on a promenade around the temple garden. This morning the sun is out, and new shoots are starting to emerge from the bare earth. I was sorely tempted. I said no – I didn't do any writing yesterday or the day before, and I was afraid that if I didn't start straight away that I'd lose resolve and pretend that other things were more important. And now here I am.

I write in the mornings because writing is generally the most difficult thing I have to do all day. There is something about the blank page which frightens the bejesus out of me, even after all these years. I put it off, I procrastinate, and I am *very* easily distracted. I write first thing, before I check my email or Facebook, because I have learnt through long and weary experience that if I don't do this, the writing doesn't get done.

Days when I have completed my morning's writing feel completely different to days when I have it yet-to-be-done. It's like walking downhill rather than uphill. Whether or not I do manage to write later in the day, I carry the fact-that-I-haven't-written with me until then and it weighs a tonne.

The same is true of days when I have a tricky unwritten email, or when I know I should have dusted the cobwebs decorating the hallway. These slightly or very unpleasant tasks sit just out of sight, taunting me, until I've done them (or, if they are big tasks, at least making a start and planning the rest into my diary).

How do we face the things we have the most resistance to? We take it very gently. We start by doing something small and then we keep going. The simplest thing that helps me is to limit the amount of time I do the task for. I usually give myself a target of an hour's writing – some people work better if they give themselves a certain number of words. If I finish and I want to carry on and do more then that's fine, but I set the target low rather than making it a stretch. I find that I'm more likely to be in a good mood and keep on working if I feel I'm achieving small things, rather than continually failing to reach my targets.

Michael Nobbs, a blogger who helps people to get their creative work done, suggests setting a timer for twenty minutes and then stopping. The stopping is important – if you've promised yourself that you're going to stop for a break and then you carry on regardless, you will learn not to trust yourself. If you stop in the middle of whatever you're doing rather than working to a natural close, you should find it easy to return after your break – you'll want to finish that sentence!

Sometimes we just have to live with the worst things without being able to do anything about them. Maybe we know we have an unpleasant meeting coming up, or a loved one is ill. It may be helpful to put some time aside to feel the feelings that accompany these worst things, or it may be helpful to get on with other things. Either way, be extra gentle with yourself when you are carrying these burdens in your heart.

Many of us easily fall into feeling that we should be doing better. On some days we do manage to tackle the thing we're most resisting, and on some days we don't. That's okay. Feel good when you manage to open the nasty letter rather than tidying your desk, or when you clean the cat bowls rather than having a mid-morning snack. Progress is more attainable and motivating than perfection. Developing these new good habits is a long term project. Have patience, and keep going.

Questions for reflection

Do you tend to do the easy or the difficult things first?

How does this work for you?

What kinds of tasks do you have the most resistance to?

What effect does this have on your life?

What would you like to prioritise that you don't currently prioritise?

What do you have the most resistance to doing right now? Could you get started on it, even if you just spent five minutes on it?

Listen to your body

Symptoms are a way of thinking about difficult things, thinking with the sound turned off.
~ Adam Phillips

What remarkable entities our bodies are. As I sit here at my desk I am pausing to consider the complexity of the movements necessary to type these words. All the while, my heart is beating, my lungs are breathing, and my stomach is digesting food. My blood is being cleaned and my eyes are translating light waves into pictures. My brain is flitting from thought to thought like a hummingbird. My body is keeping itself from slumping onto the floor like so much meat.

There is so much mystery inside of us. The scientists know many things, but there is much that remains out of reach. One of these mysteries is the relationship between the health of our body and the health of our minds.

What is my body saying right now? It is saying that the yoga I did yesterday has made it feel lighter and has also left residues of pain where I haven't attended to my muscles for a long time. My neck muscles are telling me I'm tired and stressed. My stomach says it's peckish.

We can always get more information about how we are by tuning in to our bodies. Sometimes this tuning in is curative in itself. We notice tension in our shoulders and as we continue to pay attention, our muscles relax a notch of their own accord. Sometimes we receive information that we are invited to act upon – our stomach says 'slow down!' and we realise that we have been over-scheduling ourselves and running on adrenaline.

How friendly are you with your body? This isn't just about how well we treat it – by feeding it well, giving it plenty of sleep and exercising. This is also about how often we listen to it. We can blank out our body in the way we blank out people, ignoring the after-effects of caffeine, or becoming unconscious of the nagging pain in our calf which needs attention.

Sometimes what our body has to say is inconvenient – 'I need you to rest now', or, 'I really don't like it when you eat dairy'. Our body holds wisdom about our relationships too – we feel a prickly feeling in our torso when we visit a particular friend, or we get sleepy when our partner starts speaking about what they need from us. We can choose to ignore these pointers if we want to, but we will always be missing an opportunity and there will always be a cost.

Our body is on our side. It wants us to go on walking through the world. It does its best for us, like a panting dog with its tail thumping. When it 'fails' us, it's because it has already worked so hard with the material it's been given, pushing blood through constrictions as long as it can, or processing the junk we feed it without complaint.

When your body next speaks up, take some time to wonder about what it might be saying. Say thank you to it right now, for carrying you so far already. I'm sitting here noticing the freckles and hairs on my arms, wondering at the bones moving in my fingers, my ears translating birdsong, struck dumb with awe and gratitude.

Questions for reflection

What is your body saying right now?

How well do you take care of your body? How do you feed it, rest it, give it opportunities to play or help it to repair itself?

How often do you listen to your body?

What activities (yoga, meditation etc.) help you to listen to your body?

What recurrent symptoms do you experience?

If these symptoms could speak, what might they say? What tone of voice might they use? What colour are they? If you free associate beginning with the symptoms, where does it take you?

How could you become more friendly with your body?

How could you give your body some love?

Eat art

> *If you have only two pennies, spend the first on bread and the other on hyacinths for your soul.*
> *~ Arab Proverb*

Art takes us outside of ourselves. We spend a lot of time trapped in our musty frightened little-me selves. Experiencing good art is like opening the window a crack, letting in a gulp of cool air.

Art radiates beauty, or delivers us wisdom. Sometimes it articulates something we've been struggling to make sense of, or gives us a feeling that we have been heard. Maybe it brings us hope. If we get near to the right kind of art and sit very still, it will work its magic on us.

When I say art, I don't just mean operas and Proust. I mean the pink and green birds printed on the stone placemat I'm resting my mug on. I mean dance music. I mean your neighbour's meticulously planted vegetable garden. I mean anything that has been crafted by someone with love and intent. It doesn't have to be pretty. It just has to touch parts of you that are usually out of reach.

It's good to invest some time in seeking out the forms of art that nourish us the most. For me this is poetry. Poems are like a dose of vitamins for my soul. Not all poetry, though. 95% of poetry leaves me cold. When I was younger I would ferret through anthologies, trying each poem like a chocolate from a box – no, that tastes boring. No, I don't like the ones with alcohol in. Yes, yes yes – this one is delicious. When I found one I liked I'd seek out more by that author, interested in whether it was a one-off or if they spoke a language I wanted to learn.

When I came into relationship with certain poems, an alchemical process occurred. It's a mysterious process, and I can't explain it completely. I think that these poems contained something that was only half known in me. Whether it was something in the content of the poem or something about the sound of the language, they took root at the edges of my consciousness. They grew and danced here, edging me towards the acknowledgement of some hidden wound or to a larger capacity for compassion.

To reach this, I didn't just read the poem once or twice. Very occasionally I would fall in love with a poem after a single reading, like falling in love at first sight, but mostly the relationship built more slowly. A single line would flirt with me – I would be attracted to its cadence, or its meaning would intrigue me but just elude me. I'd read it again and things might become a little clearer. I'd get to know the landscape of the poem like returning again and again to a favourite hill. The full resonance of it would slowly open up, in the way we slowly become fond of new friends.

These poems then accompany me on my journey, in the way that good friends do. They helped me in my courtship with Kaspa, when just after we'd met he went to India and we'd send each other our favourite poems. They brought me solace when pieces of my life broke. They spoke to the newly awakened spiritual me, as I returned to old favourites by Rumi and Mary Oliver with new eyes.

Good art always sends me in the direction of 'new'. It brings fresh thoughts and feelings, or intensifies those that are already lurking in me. At other times I seek safety and familiarity - detective novels or bright Saturday night television - entertainment which allows me to switch off my brain and be anaesthetised. There is a place for this, as it's impossible for us to be awake twenty four hours a day, but I don't think it's quite art. Of course, one person's entertainment is another person's art, and vice versa. Art is what pokes us, seduces us or sweetly lullabies us. Art entices us away from unconsciousness.

I tend to forget how much I love poems, and how much poems love me. When I come across one I used to have a relationship with, it sends a thrill through me. Writing this chapter has awakened something in me again. Maybe as soon as I finish, I'll get out a few of my old favourites, or maybe even order something new. What about you?

Questions for reflection

What is your equivalent of poetry? Music? Visual art? Film? Graphic comics?

How often do you spend time with your favourite art?

Which new kind of art has been flirting with you, encouraging you to spend a bit more time with it?

How could you go out on a date with some new art?

Which pieces of art (pictures, music etc.) are you grateful for? What part have they played in your life? If you enter into conversation with them again, do you think they'd have anything new to say?

What art do you avoid? Why?

What art brings you pleasure? How could you enjoy it more?

What art could you eat right now?

Do something small

> *My way of doing things is simple. It's not necessary to make impossible efforts when troubled. Put simply, when you are vexed just be vexed and say, 'Yes, and what shall I do?' Just be in suspense about the outcome and move forward a little at a time.* ~ Dr. Shoma Morita

When we are in a place of needing help, we often don't see clearly. Fog descends, and we lose our footing. Just in case you are lost in the fog, I shall now remind you of something that you already know. What helps is to break huge scary things down into teensy not-so-scary things, and then to take action, regardless of how you feel.

When we are faced with a task that feels bigger than our resources for coping with it, we become overwhelmed. The lovely word 'whelm' comes from an old English word 'whelmen', meaning 'to overturn or upset'. The word 'over' was added in Middle English to drum the point home. Overwhelm is a balloon pumped with water until the rubber is stretched to the point of bursting and beyond.

As soon as we step into the realm of overwhelm, we are not at our best. We may freeze, or we may charge at the task at hand as if we were the metaphorical bull in a china shop. We may run for the hills. We may be fogged by feelings which we either suffer through, distract ourselves from with compulsive behaviour, or push into denial. If things continue, it may reach a point where something inside us breaks.

In Alcoholics Anonymous they ask alcoholics to stop drinking one day at a time. This is very good advice. Imagine using alcohol as your primary support for decades and then being told you can never drink again – not even a single shot. If, however, you are asked to refrain from drinking just for this single day, the prospect changes. Don't think about tomorrow. Can you make it to bed time tonight without a drink?

When a day feels too long, the suggestion is that you refrain from drinking for this next hour, or maybe just for the next minute. As time ticks on, the intense craving begins to fade, and sober time begins to mount up. As this happens, other coping mechanisms are learnt, new friends are made, and a whole life changes piece by piece. It is possible to make drastic changes in circumstances that seem utterly hopeless from the perspective of all looking in – I have seen it happen. There is always hope.

So how do we break huge scary things into smaller not-so-scary things? First we need to notice when we are facing something bigger than we can handle. This can be easier said than done – huge scary things are masters of disguise. We may automatically go into 'coping mode' and only realise much later that we have been stretched past our limit. We may not think our strong feelings are justified by the circumstances and so dismiss them, leaving them to lie just out of sight, where they putrefy and grow in power.

It can help to tune into our bodies and minds and get to know the particular ways in we experience stress or overwhelm.

Do our neck muscles clench into hard fists? Does our breathing speed up? What thoughts do we have when we're staving off overwhelm? 'I'm useless at this', 'I'll be okay when...' or 'nobody ever helps me'? What are our habitual behaviours – making reams of lists, losing patience with our children, or eating more sugar?

Once you've acknowledged that, for whatever reason, you're facing overwhelm, identify the huge scary thing and then smash it into little pieces. You could start by writing everything-that-needs-doing down. Once you've chosen a first small thing to do, put the bit of paper away somewhere so it can't scare you. Alternatively you could just choose one thing (the huge scary thing's toenail) and leave the rest for now.

An example. The scary thing might be that the chaos of your flat has spiralled out of control. You could sit down for ten minutes and write a long list of everything that needs doing, or you might prefer to start by tidying the table. If thinking about tidying the whole table brings back the overwhelm, then imagine taking those two mugs back into the kitchen. Doable? Good – do it, as soon as you can. You don't have to feel joyful about it. As Dr. Shoma Morita advises, acknowledge your feelings and then do it regardless. Then decide what the next small thing is, and do that.

Achieving something small, even putting two mugs back in the kitchen, can give us a little boost of positive energy. It reminds us that we are capable of getting things done, which we almost can't imagine when we're in overwhelm. If we focus on what we are doing, it also takes our attention away from the seething morass of our own feelings. Last week I happened to feel very low immediately before a psychotherapy session with a client. I came out with my mood completely transformed. Paying close attention my client's world for fifty minutes, regardless of what I found there, released me from a preoccupation with myself and let the light back in.

We've talked about practical tasks, but what about emotional overwhelm? We all have our own patterns and habits when it comes to handling emotion. Some people will respond to emotional challenge by shutting down and withdrawing – by feeling nothing at all. Others will get grumpy or mean, or become physically unwell (somatising) or get anxious or feel depressed. We all have our preferred coping mechanisms which were set up, mostly entirely unconsciously, in our childhoods.

Changing these habits is a life-long task. Coping mechanisms are there for a good reason, so don't expect to get rid of them too quickly. Bit by bit, you can begin to unpack or untangle your behaviour. When does it happen? How does it feel? Share with a friend or in therapy or write it all down in a journal. Meditation can also help with intense emotion. If you're furious with your brother, set the timer for five minutes and as you sit, allow yourself to taste the anger as it fills you up. Don't judge it, just observe it. Notice what it feels like in your body. What colour is it? How is it moving? What thoughts arise? Let them go and keep breathing. At the end of the five minutes, get up and engage with something different as a way of putting your attention onto something else. If we are able to take the position of observer when strong emotion arrives, it allows us to step back from being entirely inside the emotion.

Sometimes we feel overwhelmed by tasks or situations in a way that doesn't make any sense. At these times others might tell us to just pull ourselves together, or we berate ourselves, telling ourselves to stop being so silly. In my experience, we're never randomly afraid or angry. They may be outdated, but our brains have their reasons. If we were bitten by a dog when were small our brains will arrange for us to feel a lot of fear when we see dogs, even though we know rationally that they're not going to hurt us. The fear may not be necessary, but our brains think they are protecting us. This works in more complex ways too – maybe we feel jealous of women who (unconsciously) remind us of our sisters, or we self-sabotage because being successful led us to be ridiculed when we were at school.

Sometimes it helps to try and make sense of what the underlying fear might be. Sometimes we get nowhere with it. Either way, we can accept that there will be a good reason for the fear somewhere, and then get on with breaking the situation down and taking one small action. See yourself as a frightened child who needs a lot of encouragement and support. You could even talk to yourself out loud – 'I know you're afraid to have a look at the mess your accounts are in, Satya. Here's a plan. Spend ten minutes starting to put your receipts in order, and then come back to the rest after a cup of tea. How's that?'

If you can't work out how to break the task down, or where you should begin, then it's time to ask for help. Otherwise, choose one small thing, and just begin.

Questions for reflection

When do you tend to experience overwhelm? What are your triggers?

How can you catch yourself when you're falling towards overwhelm? What happens in your body or in your mind? What compulsive behaviours do you turn towards?

How do you best break things down into small parts? Does it help to write it down? Do you cut things into small enough pieces?

How can you remember 'one day at a time'?

Do you ask for help often enough when you need it? If not, why not? Who could you ask?

What are you avoiding right now?

What small thing can you do next?

Embrace dependency

> *The myth of self-sufficiency demands optimism without end, downplays life's challenges, and shames us when, inevitably, we fall short.*
> ~ Ashton Applewhite

I have heard people say that when clients become dependent on their therapist, this is A Bad Thing. They believe therapists exploit clients by fostering dependency – as a way of securing regular income, or to get the ego-propping reassurance of being valuable to the client. They think it undermines the client's ability to discover their own answers, and to find their own way in the world once the therapy has ended.

I understand these fears, and as therapists it is our duty to investigate the dynamics in the therapy room as a continuous practice, including scrutinising our motivations. I disagree that it is always unhelpful for clients to become dependent on the therapy or on their therapist. I am familiar with this phenomenon from both sides – both as therapist and as client.

Being able to lean in to my third therapist, Sheila, and trusting her to be okay as I entered more deeply into my grief, was one of the most precious things she gave me. I didn't reach this point with my previous therapists, and although we did good work together I kept myself self-contained and safe. I trusted Sheila to hold my pain without turning away, and I also trusted her enough to miss her when she was on holiday, and to feel a deep sadness when she retired part-way through our work together. I was dependent on her, and I got hurt as a result. I am grateful for that hurt, because it showed me that it was possible to trust another human being, and that when Sheila didn't perfectly meet my needs (by postponing her retirement by another two years or so!) we talked about it, and I survived. She showed me that intimacy was possible, and I went on to find new levels of intimacy with my friends and with my future husband.

A flower would never suggest to another flower that it wasn't or shouldn't be dependent. The luminous orange marigolds outside my office window are each supported by the earth around their roots. They are fed by nutrients in the soil, and they rely on bees to pollinate them so they can produce seeds. If the rain stopped, they would die.

As human beings we are no different. One of the few things we can depend on in life is the fact that we are dependent. We are not only physically dependent on the ground under our feet, the food we eat and the medicines we are given, but we are cognitively, emotionally and spiritually dependent too. We hold reams of information in our head which is necessary for our survival – we received this from our parents and from the many generations of biologists, engineers, physicists, philosophers etc. who came before us. We were shown how to be in a relationship by our mother, spending our first nine months inside her, and then later from our father, siblings, and many others, including those we meet in books and in films. Most of us step onto the spiritual path after meeting another human being who is further along than we are, or through hearing or reading teachings from thousands of years ago.

Most of us shrink from dependency and intimacy. Even those people we think of as needy often choose partners who are unavailable – if their partner happens to change their dance and move towards them, they run away. We avoid dependency because it is terrifying! Most of us have tried that exercise in drama classes where we close our eyes and lean backwards, trusting that our partner is there, unseen, ready to catch us. This is how it is to be dependent. We are off-balance, and we teeter into the unknown. Will we be caught? Will the other use our dependency against us in the future? Will they reject us once they've seen our vulnerability? Will we get used to it and forget how to stand on our own feet, leaving us at their mercy forever?

Dependency is terrifying, but it also brings us wonderful things. Nick Totton speaks up for dependency in his book, Not a Tame Lion. He reminds the therapists he is addressing that, "We are in a position to know that *depending on someone who is dependable* is a healing experience, allowing enormous relief of tension, relaxation from the often unconscious sense that one is all alone and that nothing and no one can be relied on." This is also true when we can bring ourselves to rely on the natural world, letting the earth support us as we look up at the clouds, or when we rely on our version of God. The second and third steps of the Twelve Steps of Alcoholics Anonymous are coming to believe that there is something out there that we can lean on, and then leaning on it.

Along with this great sense of relief, an honest look at our dependency can also lead to gratitude. We have a spiritual exercise in our Amida Shu Buddhist tradition called Nei Quan where we spend some time reflecting on three questions, the first of which is what we have received over the past twenty-four hours. This exercise points us towards the reality of our dependent natures, and as people remember the car that took them to work, the boiler that's heating the room they're sitting in, the colleague who made them a cup of tea, they often realise how much they receive in every moment.

So if dependency is inevitable, deeply healing and scary, how do we negotiate it more gracefully? This is a life's work! We can slowly learn to tell the difference between healthy and unhealthy dependency. Feeling dependent on our bullying boss as we need the money is not healthy. Relying on any one person for our sense of self-esteem is not healthy. What about relying on our husband to do all the driving? What about a fiery friendship that brings us much joy and much heartache? Relationships are rarely straightforwardly 'healthy' or 'unhealthy', and often change over time. How can we lean deeply into our dependency, but also know that we will be okay if we do fall?

The antidote to fearful dependency is always more faith. When we've had enough of our bullying boss we might decide to leave, trusting that we will find another job, or that even if we don't we'll somehow manage to feed ourselves and to be okay. This 'being okay' doesn't mean that we get what we want, or that we don't suffer. It is somehow larger than the suffering – we can bear it, we trust that we will survive it. We lean into the world again, gingerly, as if our bones have broken, and we trust that we will heal. We hold onto the glimmer of light we see out the corner of our eyes, and we wait. As my Buddhist teacher

Dharmavidya says, 'I'm not okay, you're not okay, and that's okay'.

Questions for reflection

What are you dependent on? Write a list.

Who are you dependent on? Write a list.

How is it to write or to look at these lists?

Where would you rather not be dependent?

When have you had a bad experience of being dependent in the past? What has this left you with?

When have you had a good experience of being dependent?

How can you choose more healthy forms of dependency?

How can you shift some of your demands of the world and of others into requests?

Does your dependency and what you receive ever connect you to gratitude?

Where can you rest?

Find fellow feeling

> *You come to realize that, yeah, this is the kind of guy I am: insensitive, uncaring, unthinking—a real bastard most of the time. Recognizing that that is really what you are helps you to stop beating other people over the head for their imperfections. And that's compassion. ~ Rev. Dr. Alfred Bloom*

Sometimes life is difficult. No-one is there for us, and no-one understands. We are on our own with our own mix of fear, pain and hopelessness. We are the hatchling who has fallen too early from the nest and lies without feathers on the hard ground.

Paradoxically, this feeling of being alone is something that we all share. It is, as Terrance Keenan reminds us in the book's epigraph, how we begin. As we remember that there are others in the world who feel as we do, something in us begins to unfurl; the delicate tip of a fern, reaching out towards the light. Our husband had a disturbed night. Maybe we could offer him a cup of coffee. Or we could fuss our dog for a while. Maybe we could walk in the garden and hold our loneliness up against the shy hellebore, or recognise our longing in the misty horizon.

We have more in common than we think we do. We are all travelling in the same boat or, if you prefer, our boats all have leaks. We can connect with fellow feeling by stripping off some of our protective layers and remembering what's inside.

We all need to sleep, defecate, and urinate. We all have bodies that get cold or hot, that will wrinkle up, and that break down more often as time goes on. We all want to be liked. We all lose the things that we love. We have all woken up in the dark corners of the night and felt frightened.

We can forget that our deepest vulnerabilities are known to others as most of us do our best to hide them. We hide them from others and we hide them from ourselves. We paste on our cheerful smile before we step out of our front door. We post photos of our children looking beautiful on Facebook. We ignore the anxious fluttering in our stomach and pay attention instead to the television or work or anything else we can lay our hands on. We are ashamed of our desires, our failings and our meanness. Some of us are afraid of our beauty and our strength. We are all involved in a continual PR campaign and none of us see the whole picture.

In order to find fellow feeling, we need to see deep inside ourselves as well as inside others. How do we do that? We find fellow feeling by listening carefully. We listen to each other and we listen to ourselves. We find friends with sympathetic ears, and quiet spaces. We also listen to God – Good, Humanity, Nature, Buddha, The Universe, or anything that is bigger and wiser than you. Put some time aside to listen to the small birds and the echoing train yards. Do whatever it is that comes closest to praying for you. Light a candle and pay attention to the silence between sounds. Open your heart. Let new wisdom in. We are always alone, and we are never alone. Fellow feeling reminds us of this, and gives us a reason to reach out towards others. When we reach out, the whole world reaches back. I hope you can take its hand.

Questions for reflection

When did you last feel fellow feeling? What arose in you next?

When is it easy for you to have fellow feeling for those around you? When do you struggle?

When do you feel most alone?

What spaces in your life do you have where you are listened to? How might you find more?

When do you listen properly to others? What tends to get in the way of listening to the other?

What can you hear right now when you listen to yourself? What can you hear from the Universe?

Surrender control

> *This is not your week to run the Universe. Next week is not looking so good either.* ~ Susan J. Elliott

Ah, running the Universe. My favourite job. Everything goes so smoothly when I'm in charge. People get along with each other, projects finish on time and successfully, I get to do exactly what I want, and it all just feels so safe and comfortable.

Granted, it is a little tiring. Especially because of all those people who keep on getting it wrong. And when I correct them, they don't always do exactly what I say. Come to think of it, it's not just other people who don't obey me. The weather doesn't listen to me much either. Or money. Or my cats (especially my cats). Or those parts of myself that rebel and send out orders to eat cake, even when I've clearly told them not to. Or my body...

Okay, I surrender. Have you surrendered yet? Where are you still clinging onto control?

It's not surprising that we enjoy being in control, or at least enjoy the illusion that we're in control. The world is so unpredictable! How are we meant to protect ourselves, or get more of what we like, or keep the nasty stuff away? How are we meant to make plans? How are we meant to deal with the fact that other people make up their own minds?

I have a clear memory of a sunny day when I was a small girl. Some older children I didn't know were staying with us, and we were all engaged in an important project – tidying the summer house. I really needed the toilet, but I was reluctant to go down the long path back to the house – there was still so much to do. What I did was leave the older children with very clear instructions about what they should be doing while I was away, delivered in a very loud voice. There was to be no negotiation. Even now I can remember the sense of satisfaction that this gave me, and how delicious the power tasted. It was as if they had become extensions of my own body, doing the things I wanted to do myself but without any expenditure of effort.

This juicy feeling was the start of a long career in bossiness ('a skill for directing' might be a kinder way to put it). This is one trait amongst a host of strategies I have in order to take control. I am efficient and I get lots done. I use charm and charisma to manipulate others. I am highly organised. I have occasional emotional meltdowns so those close to me will rescue me. Et cetera. I'm guessing that you will be able to make your own list of the things you do to manipulate the world.

Of course, all of these methods are all doomed to fail sooner or later. However cleverly I manipulate powerful people into liking me, they are left with a sense of me not quite being authentic, or they want to be seen as who they are rather than just as tickets to something I want. When the items on my to-do list exceed the time I have available, I organise myself into a frenzy before having one of the afore-mentioned meltdowns which, even when I am rescued, leave me feeling disappointed with myself and guilty for having dragged other people into my mess.

There is an alternative. Whether life forces us to, or whether we come to see the wisdom in choosing to, we can surrender our control. We were never really in control in the first place – more accurately we are surrendering our illusion of control. Surrender doesn't mean becoming passive victims or making excuses for cowardice. Sometimes it is correct to take action. Surrendering control means letting go of trying to direct the whole play, and instead playing only the part we have been given. The Serenity Prayer helps us with this:

> *God grant me the serenity to accept the things I cannot change*
> *Courage to change the things I can*
> *And the wisdom to know the difference*

Of course, knowing the difference takes a lifetime of practice. As a general rule, especially when it comes to relationships, the thing we can change (sometimes!) is ourselves. We can do this by taking responsibility, by saying yes or no, by improving our self-knowledge, by fostering fellow feeling etc. The things we are powerless over, as Alcoholics Anonymous puts it, are 'people, places and things'. We may not be powerless to our *reactions* to people, places and things, but we can't do very much at all about who or what they are. Seeing the truth of this can feel terrifying, and it can also feel like a great relief.

This feeling of relief is what I'd like to offer you more than anything. When you realise how little you actually are in control of, you can relax! Other people probably won't fall apart if you stop doing all those things you do to 'maintain' them or to keep them from harm. If they do, it isn't your fault. They have 'three C's' in Al-Anon: you didn't cause the alcoholic to drink, you can't control their drinking, and you can't cure it. Give other people the dignity of making their own mistakes, and bring your attention back to all the ones you're still making. Let your fingers unclasp, one by one. Take a deep breath. Let the ocean of light and love hold you.

Questions for reflection

How could you apply the Serenity Prayer to your own life at the moment?

Where do you cling to control?

How do you think being in control will make you feel? How does it actually make you feel?

Where would you like to release control? What are you afraid might happen if you did?

What would be the worst case scenario if you relinquished control?

When have you let go of control in the past? What happened?

Who can you hand your control over to? Other people? The Universe?

Can you feel any of the relief I'm talking about in this chapter? Can you imagine that you might feel it in the future?

What would you like to let go of right now?

Grow gratitude

> *Again I resume the long*
> *lesson: how small a thing*
> *can be pleasing, how little*
> *in this hard world it takes*
> *to satisfy the mind*
> *and bring it to its rest.*
> *~ Wendell Berry*

Gratitude leads us to kneel down before small and large pleasing things and let tears come to our eyes. Gratitude points towards the myriad things we have received, rather than looking wistfully at the list of all the things we want. Gratitude helps us to taste the good stuff, and opens us up to receive more of it.

Earlier I mentioned a spiritual exercise called Nei Quan. This involves sitting quietly and asking ourselves three questions – 'Over the past twenty four hours what have I received, what have I offered in return and what trouble has my existence caused?' We are encouraged to list as many concrete examples from each category as we can, especially the first. Here's what I come up with when I try it right now:

What have I received? This morning Kaspa spent two hours fixing the internet. As I read in bed yesterday evening I was visited by a purring cat. I have just eaten two jam tarts made with pastry made by someone in a factory, and jam made from cherries. Someone planted the cherry trees, harvested them, boiled them into jam. I listened to some beautiful music which someone spent a lot of time creating. I have used my computer to type this chapter, and the electricity that comes into my wall from goodness knows where. We did some yoga this morning following a free video from a great yoga teacher. I received payment from a psychotherapy client. My body has carried me around, my blood has cleaned itself, my heart has been beating...

What have I offered in return? I thanked Kaspa. I posted a short teaching on our virtual temple. I texted a friend and said I hoped she had a good day. I washed my cat's bowls and fed them. I listened to my psychotherapy client.

What trouble has my existence caused? I consumed food that someone else could have eaten. It cost money to heat this building I live in, to light it, to keep the plumbing going. I lost my patience with Kaspa. I forgot to let my bunnies out for their exercise.

You can see that the first list is much longer than the second. And I could have easily written more on the third. The idea of Nei Quan is that it illustrates in a very concrete way our dependent natures as human beings. It reminds us of how much we receive without asking for it and how little we offer in return. We will never be able to 'repay' our parents for the many hours they spent feeding, clothing and cleaning us when we were very small. We are supported in every breath by the air around us and in every step by the ground under our feet. We depend utterly on other people and on water and on the sun.

Nei Quan can be one window onto gratitude. There are others. Some of us are lucky enough to have a greater capacity for gratitude than others, but that doesn't mean we can't get better at it. Mostly we need to practice paying attention to what we receive, whether or not we feel grateful, and trust that the feeling will follow. List ten things you can be grateful for at the end of every day, or ask a friend to remind you what you receive. Pause once a day to find a *small stone*, a written-down moment of accurate observation, or find three beautiful things in your environment. Spend some time reflecting on the care your parents gave you when you were a baby – regardless of the other ways they may have neglected or damaged you, they must have fed you enough for you to stay alive, changed your clothes, carried you with them, taken you to the doctor when you needed to go…

We may be avoiding the feeling of gratitude. We may be afraid of facing the truth of our deep dependency on other people and things. We may be holding tightly onto our resentments, because we know who we are with our resentments, and we don't want to feel our grief as we let our expectations go. We might be resolutely closed to the possibility that what we want isn't the same as what we need.

Relax: nothing is under control. Let gratitude soften you and lean back into the not-knowing. Know that when we taste gratitude properly, it always leaves us humbled, full of thanks, and often moist-eyed. It shows us how we can lean in to the world and be held, and it shows us the abundance of what we receive, even when we don't feel the abundance.

Pluck the fruit of gratefulness – it's all around us, plump and ripe. Taste it.

Questions for reflection

How often do you feel grateful?

How does gratitude affect you?

When do you find it most difficult to be grateful?

How might you be clinging on to feelings of ingratitude? Why do you think you might be doing this?

What would you like to do to strengthen your gratitude muscles?

Who or what would you like to say thank you to right now? Do it.

Hand it over

> *Cast all your anxiety on him because he cares for you.* ~ 1 Peter 5:7 (NIV)

When someone is upset with me, my tendency is to take full responsibility for their upset. Feelings of guilt persist even after I've examined my own side carefully and apologised for anything I feel I've done unskilfully. I can get stuck going over and over what's happened, desperate to fix the other person and fix myself.

This is one of the habitual patterns that I struggle with. Other things in my life keep coming back to haunt me too – a tendency to worry about finances, a propensity to workaholism, feelings around not being successful enough. Whether these issues return to me of their own accord or whether I pick them up myself, it soon becomes clear that I'm not making much progress with them. There's a sense of déjà vu – the feelings are very familiar, or my thoughts circle. Sometimes I feel so overwhelmed that it's difficult to concentrate on anything else.

When this happens, I try to make a conscious decision to hand it all over. As a Buddhist, I hand things over to the Buddha. I imagine him sitting serenely with a big golden table in front of him, and I see myself placing whatever it is (my worries, my fear, my circling thoughts) on the table. His hands are always open, and he always receives everything with a smile.

I usually feel an instant sense of relief. I don't have to lie awake at night worrying about my colleague, because the Buddha is looking after her. I don't have to keep searching for a solution for that problem, because the Buddha is taking care of it for me. When I pick them back up again, as soon as I realise (like looking down to find a spoon in my hand that I'd forgotten I was moving from room to room) I just hand them back to the Buddha. Sometimes I take them back from his table many times, as he sits there patiently with an amused glint in his eye!

Handing things over is a way to remind ourselves that we're not responsible for the Universe, or even for one other person. When our worries overwhelm us, as well as feeling awful we can become incapable of thinking creatively or of seeing a way out. Handing our problems over reminds us that we don't have to carry them on our own. It reminds us that we can receive help if we allow ourselves to ask. We can place our burden down in a safe place and rest for a while.

When I hand problems over in this way I find that, if I'm patient, a solution will appear when I least expect it. This doesn't mean that we stop taking responsibility for ourselves, or that we don't take any necessary action. If we are looking for a job, we don't stop looking in the papers and filling out applications. We carry on doing the leg work, but we let go of the results – we leave our anxieties with the Buddha and we trust that things will turn out okay in the end. We open our minds to the possibility that the solution that's best for us might not be the same as the one we want. We cling a little less tightly to controlling it all.

What if you're not Buddhist? I think the Buddha would be happy to receive your burdens anyway – his golden table is infinite. Otherwise, any kind of Higher Power works for this exercise – God, Good, The Universe. The point is to prise the problem out of your sticky hands for a while, and I like to think of it being kept somewhere safe. It's generally more effective to imagine something outside of yourself, but you might prefer to hand it over to your own unconscious to work on. Give it a try a few times and see whether it's something that works for you.

Handing things over is a relatively new thing for me to do. For most of my life I sought safety by putting more and more effort into influencing other people and the world, and so the idea of letting things go is scary. It's only through repeated experience that I've come to rely on it. It helps me in a practical way, by bringing me fresh solutions and by allowing me to focus my attention back onto my own business. More importantly, it makes me feel better – less alone, less overwhelmed, and more full of hope. I hope it will help you too.

Questions for reflection

When do you tend to become overwhelmed? What triggers you?

How do you feel about the idea of handing things over?

Who or what might you hand your problems over to? How could you visualise this?

When you practice handing something over, how does it feel?

How patient are you when you are waiting for solutions?

How open minded are you when you're looking for solutions?

What do you need to hand over right now?

Structures support us

> *In limits, there is freedom. Creativity thrives within structure.* ~ Julia Cameron

My teacher Dharmavidya tells a story about a Korean master who led a highly and tightly structured life. He had to move quickly from one appointment to another, all of them organised by someone else. When asked how he coped with it, he said that he 'only did exactly what he wanted to do'. How can we make any sense of this?

In my own life, I have discovered that it is helpful for me to develop structures, systems and rules which support me in my work and play. When the systems are running smoothly, I am much less likely to worry about things or get caught up in dithering. I feel settled and focussed, and I approach my work with the same lightness I feel when I wake up to a day without appointments at the weekend.

Many of us have associations between structures and being suffocated. Maybe we resented being told what to do at school, or having to do chores at home. Maybe we think that structures are always forcing us to do the things we don't want to do. As I sit here right now, I am feeling almost overwhelmed by an urge to get up and eat a jam tart. I know that they are sitting in a tin just in the other room, and I have a craving for sugar. I have also had a very distracted morning, not getting down to my writing, browsing the web and avoiding what I planned to do.

Isn't freedom going to eat the jam tart? No – it's the opposite. Eating the jam tart is obeying a single noisy urge that rises up in me, whether or not I think it's good idea. It's becoming a hostage to the compulsions that prevent me from getting things done. The things I want to get done, like writing, are important to me. And so here I am, still typing, with the jam tart urge still tugging at my skirt.

Structures offer me a wonderful support, like allowing my head to be cradled by strong hands. They remove the necessity of making decisions on a moment to moment basis, which gives those jam tart urges a lots of gaps to sneak in. Some of these structures I have initiated myself, like always cleaning the cat bowls before I do anything else in the mornings, and some of them have been agreed in joint decisions or suggested by others, like having a regular meeting with Kaspa on a Thursday morning. They all have a good purpose behind them, and they keep me on track.

I only recently realised that structures are helpful for my rest time too. Kaspa and I had started another of our rest days setting off in the car to seek some kind of entertainment. After an aimless and dissatisfying morning, we realised that we needed to put more effort into planning our time off, without turning it into a day of commitments. We'd confused unstructured time with rest time, and had thought that any appointments would put pressure on us.

We made a list of some things that we enjoyed doing together – following a yoga video, doing some gentle gardening, eating lunch out, going on walks – and we made sure we had more of a plan for what to do when we had our Sabbath days. Sometimes this plan is simply 'lounge around the house and read'. Yesterday we had a very different experience of our day off. Even with a few pre-booked appointments it was much more spacious, much more satisfying, and much more nourishing.

Structures are our friends. They are branches for our leaves, cutlery drawers for our cutlery, and the music for our dancing. They take a million choices out of our hands and offer us just one – will I stay here and do my writing as I have planned to do, or will I go and eat a jam tart? It's not always an easy decision, but I am committed to my freedom, and I am committed to doing the things that I want to do. At least for now, I'm staying put.

Questions for reflection

Where does structure work well to support you in your life at the moment?

What areas of your life are working less well? Where does it feel chaotic?

Where or when are you most easily distracted?

Which impulses are the ones that tend to de-rail you?

When do you tend to rebel?

What new structures could you implement which would support you to negotiate these rocky terrains more smoothly?

What would you like to do more of? How might structures help you to achieve that?

What new structure would you like to implement right now?

Make space to create

> *Making your unknown known is the important thing – and keeping the unknown always beyond you – catching – crystallizing your simpler clearer vision of life – only to see it turn stale compared to what you vaguely feel ahead – that you must always keep working to grasp...* ~ *Georgia O'Keeffe*

Finding space to be creative is crucial to our well-being. Why is this? I'm not sure. I just felt tempted to dive into the internet for answers – other people will already have written about it and I can do some copy and pasting. Then I remembered that I am writing about creativity. Creativity is when something comes out of us that couldn't come out of anyone else. We can go to a supermarket for a packet of biscuits, and some of them are very nice, but there is nothing like the smell of freshly baking cookies and the unique shapes and flavours that come out of our own ovens.

So what is my answer to why creativity is good for us? I know that being creative feeds me. I mainly exercise my creative muscles in the arena of words, and it is a mysterious process. I have told people for many years that writing is simultaneously the most important and the most difficult thing I do in my life. Sometimes I do take pleasure from the crafting process – messing about with sentences or plucking just the right word from the ether – and it is very satisfying to hold a completed book in my hands. Mostly, though, writing ranges from feeling 'just average' to being a very hard slog indeed. So why do I expend all this effort to get words on the page when I resist it so strongly, and when it can be such a tortuous process?

Is it because I feel that the world needs to hear what I'm saying? Of course, it's wonderful that some people do want to read what I write, and this is a part of my motivation for writing – both altruistically, because it helps them, and egoistically, because the praise makes me feel good. But this isn't the whole story. I write because there are ideas and stories that are queuing up to come out of me. In the process of writing them down, I clarify things to myself and I work things out that I hadn't known before. I see the world through new eyes.

I think that this is my answer to the question. Why is it good for us to be creative? Yes, it can be fun. Yes, it can bring others pleasure. But creativity is good for us because it allows us to get to know ourselves, others and the world in a new way. It shows us what we hadn't been able to see. It connects the dots. It brings us into a closer relationship with everything, so we can snuggle up to it, or learn from it, and offer it our love.

What sorts of things am I including when I speak about creating? I'm including the strawberry tarts you made last week, and the bulbs you laid out on the flower bed and slotted into the earth. I mean the little vase of flowers you arranged for your friend when she came to stay, and the costume you made for your daughter's school play. Anything you produce is an act of creation, however humble or insignificant you might feel it is.

How do we encourage our creativity? Joseph Campbell suggests that "Awe is what moves us forwards". We follow our noses, our curiosity, and our impulses. We look at what other people have created and we learn about our individual taste. We sign up for a tester class, or get a book out of the library. We put one foot in front of the other and we keep walking.

I would like to inflame you with an urge to make art. I don't care what – get out your watercolours, bake blue cupcakes, write *small stones*, arrange autumn leaves into a pattern on the grass. See if you can lose yourself in the crafting. See if you can find pleasure in the process, and withstand the frustration and self-doubt and fear that almost inevitably accompanies art-making. Don't be afraid. Share whatever you make with others – they will take joy in seeing your creations. See what can learn about yourself and about the world. Make art! Make art! Make art!

Questions for reflection

In what areas of your life are you already creative? Don't discount anything too quickly.

What do you tell yourself about how creative you are?

What kinds of products of creativity do you enjoy consuming? If you love clothes, do you fancy making them? If you love chocolates, do you want to buy some chocolate moulds?

What art do you like to look at? What music do you like to listen to? Which gardens do you appreciate? Where else can you draw inspiration?

Can you remember the last time you got lost in creating something? How was it?

If you weren't worried about how good it might be, what kind of art might you try making?

How can you make a little space to make something this week or month?

Is there anyone who would like to make something with you? A friend who'd join a knitting circle with you? You could do some painting with your son?

How can you look at making art with more lightness?

What tiny creative act can you do right now?

Everything changes

*Since my house burned down
I now own a better view
of the rising moon.
~ Mizuta Masahide*

Everything changes. As we say in one of our morning verses, 'impermanence rushes upon us every moment'. The autumn leaves are on their way out, as they drift down and fragment into the earth. I watch our old arthritic cat walk across the room. The Malvern Hills that stand behind the temple came into being around 680 million years ago. Maybe in another few hundred million years they might wear away to nothing. Sometimes things change very slowly, but everything changes.

As human beings we resist a full knowledge of this change, wanting instead to rest in the assurance of knowing-where-we-are. We like to think of ourselves as constant and predictable, and we prefer to see other people, places and things as constant too.

When we're not able to face change as it happens, we become stuck in the past: petrified. We waste energy complaining about things not being as they once were, or we go into denial and act in ways that don't match the current reality. A parent might struggle to treat their son as an adult, or an ailing woman might continue working at the same frantic pace she's always worked at, even though her body is screaming at her to slow down. We can't escape change, and it doesn't help us in the long run when we try to.

Sometimes it is a comfort to remember that everything changes. "This too shall pass." When we're in the jaws of a tortuous situation it can feel as if it will never end – and yet even the process of dying is a journey with an ever-changing landscape, both physically and emotionally. If we can't bear for something to go on forever, we can relax a little and remember that it won't.

The Buddha spoke about impermanence in his fundamental teaching The Three Marks or Signs of Being. This consists of three lines of three words each, written below in Sanskrit:

> *sarva samskara anitya*
> *sarva samskara dukkha*
> *sarva dharma anatma*

Sarva means all. *Samskara* can be translated as mental formations or confections – the stories we tell about the world, which are all clotted with self-reference. Thus the first statement holds that all of our confections contain *anitya*, or impermanence, and the second that all our confections contain *dukkha*, or dissatisfaction. The third switches to the word *dharma* which can be translated as 'objects with or without self', 'things as they are' or the truth. *Anatma* means without-self. Thus the third statement, 'all truth is without self', is suggesting that we only encounter the truth when we allow things to be 'things as they are' rather than 'things as we see them'. As my teacher Dharmavidya puts it, "I suggest that this text tells us that the stories we tell ourselves – which are redolent with self-reference – are ephemeral and cause trouble and that the truth has nothing to do with self."

How might this teaching help us face the inevitability of change? After making this interpretation of the text, Dharmavidya goes on to say that "Liberation and nirvana are the result of deeply realising this and having faith in it." What is it we can deeply realise? That there is no way of avoiding change or suffering. What can we have faith in? That there is a kind of truth that exists outside of our self-coloured experience of the world, and that this is somewhere we can rest. We can find this rest by letting go of our clinging-to-self, and allowing grace to enter us. I think this is what Teresa of Avila is referring to in her beautiful exhortation: "Let nothing disturb you. Let nothing frighten you. Everything passes away except God."

Regardless of whether we have an intuition of this transcendent truth or not, we can lean into the first two statements. We imagine that we will never survive the battering power of the grief we feel. We imagine the intensity will go on forever. However slowly it abates, like the hills that stand behind me, it will change. We can't avoid dissatisfaction, but it will stay continually fresh, shifting and transmogrifying as we are swept along by the river of life. If we can find peace in the midst of change, nothing will frighten us. We can let the water support us and carry us forwards.

Questions for reflection

Is there anything currently in your life that you are afraid will never change?

If you look back, can you remember a time when you thought something would never change? Did it?

What happens when you pay closer attention to something that seems like it's not moving?

If you are feeling impatient for something to change, how can you be more patient?

Where in your life at the moment are you not facing up to change?

Which of your stories about yourself, others and the world are especially full of self-reference? How could you shift to seeing the situation more from a position of things-as-they-are?

Can you intuit a beauty in the inevitability of change?

Do you have any sense of somewhere you can rest?

Hold on

> *I begin to understand that when things fall apart it doesn't mean they're broken, it means they are forming themselves into other things.*
> *~ Patrick Lane*

Sometimes words on a page are not enough. Nothing is enough – we have been broken. We have lost our most beloved sweetheart, or our life's work is in pieces, or a child has died, or the demons that torment us have smashed us to the floor. We cannot imagine a future. We cannot imagine feeling hope again.

I wish I could make it easier for you. I wish I could take some of your pain from you for a little while, just to give you a rest. I wish I could promise you that everything will be okay. The truth is, sometimes things do get better, and sometimes they don't. There isn't always a happy ending. And yet. If you can just hang on for a bit longer, anything is possible.

I was approached at an Alcoholics Anonymous convention once by a smart looking man in a suit who presented me with a dog-eared photo. The man in the photo was so derelict, so near to death, that I didn't recognise him as the man before me, and that of course was the point. As he showed people his photo, he could hardly believe it himself. In Patrick Lane's memoir he describes how he finally got sober at the age of sixty two. He had been dependent on alcohol and cocaine for his whole life. He wanders round his garden in shock and awe, watching leaves funnelling the glistening rain, finding a tiny green frog, taking it all in through clean eyes, the fresh beauty rushing through him.

Sometimes our lives have to get very dark before we can see the light. We all experience these times when the light breaks through – the day we finally decided to stop smoking, or leave an abusive relationship, or take up painting. Sometimes these turnarounds lead us to change our behaviour forever, but more often we relapse, going back to our old habits, hoping things will turn out differently this time. It may be that, as a therapist told my friend once, we 'haven't felt enough pain yet'. We cling to our comforts and to the habits that helped us feel safe, as if our lives depended on them. As it did for Lane, sometimes it takes many decades before we hit our rock bottom – the place where we really can't sink any lower. At this point we can rest for a while on the hard floor, maybe near death, and surrender. We may think that surrendering will finish us off, but it actually allows us to accept the help we need. We are willing to do anything! We invite the Universe to do what it needs to do, and it does. We let ourselves be lifted back up towards the light.

In dark times, we often feel like we're the only one feeling this particular shade of heartbreak or confusion or desolation. The good news is that we're all in the same boat, sailing across these unpredictable and sometimes turbulent waters. Someone out there is feeling a very similar colour of feeling to yours, right now. Most of us, if you were able to describe it to us, would recognise it. Others have felt almost exactly like this, have suffered like you, and have come through it. We are never as alone as we think we are. Although it may be the last thing you want to do, try reaching out. Pick up the phone. Let someone you trust know how you're feeling.

At desolate times like these it also helps to take things one day at a time, and sometimes one hour or even one minute at a time. If you can't imagine facing a week of feeling like this, then look at the hour in front of you instead. How can you nurse yourself through the next sixty minutes? Maybe you could make yourself a hot drink, or run a bath. Maybe go outside, lie down on the grass and look up at the sky. Maybe give yourself over to crying for now, deciding when you'll stop and go for a walk.

Aim to look after yourself as you would your child or loved one if they were suffering as you are. Keep yourself showered, well fed and watered, and get enough sleep. Don't expect things to change overnight and trust the process. Ask for help. Pray. Defer making any big decisions. Write in your journal, and go out for short walks. Seek professional help if you are out of your depth. It may also help to eat chocolate.

Things do change – we can depend on that. It may be that this experience is breaking you down so it can reform you into an entirely new shape – softening you, connecting you to the tender heart of the world. It may be that we won't manage to make that change in this lifetime, but our story will continue to unfold in the people who love us and the people we've loved. The work we've begun and the love we've planted, however insufficient we might judge it to be, will bear fruit in time. If you don't have any faith right now, you can borrow mine. Just hold on.

When your day is long
And the night
The night is yours alone
When you're sure you've had enough
Of this life
Well hang on...
~ Berry, Stipe, Buck and Mills

Questions for reflection

Have there been times in your past when you felt you wouldn't get through? Did you?

Have you met anyone who found hope when they never expected to?

What help do you need? How can you seek it?

How could you look after yourself over the next week? Day? Hour?

Is there someone you know who's going through a hard time? Would you like to give them this chapter to read? What small thing could you do for them?

What small thing would help you right now? Can you go and do it (or ask someone for it) when you've finished reading?

Keep walking

Keep walking, though there's no place to get to. Don't try to see through the distances. That's not for human beings. Move within, but don't move the way fear makes you move. ~ Rumi

Yesterday I didn't write a word of this manuscript, because I had a wobble. I read what I'd written the day before and thought, 'what rubbish'. I wondered who the hell I thought I was to give advice to anyone. I saw what I'd written as simplistic, patronising, and clumsily put.

I've already put off writing for two hours this morning, and what finally helped me to sit down at my desk, close down Facebook and get typing was the thought 'it's just a wobble'.

We all have our own variety of wobbles. Some people might lose their temper, and some might slide into a grey depression. We have health wobbles and emotional wobbles, confidence wobbles and competence wobbles. Sometimes 'wobble' is an insufficient word for the sheer size of the obstruction we encounter. Sometimes we fall face-down into the mud and we can't imagine ever getting up again.

I like to fantasize about finding a way of eliminating future wobbles. Thus far, I haven't had much luck with this. I have written seven books now, and at some point during each one I was convinced that they were the worst thing ever to have been written by a human being. I had hoped that by the time I got to my third or fifth book these crises of confidence would have faded away – I've had success with my previous books, and I know that this wobbling happens – but if anything they got worse.

Everybody loses their way from time to time. It is unavoidable. Sometimes wobbles visit us less frequently, and sometimes we do get better at avoiding particular potholes, but as long as we are alive we will trip up from time to time.

Although I don't like this fact, it also helps me to feel better. I remember that wobbles happen because I am a bombu human being, not because I am a complete and utter failure. This brings some ease to the situation, dilutes its catastrophic quality, and allows me to relax.

It does also help to remind myself of previous wobbles. In the middle of my last book I remember feeling pretty much exactly how I do now. I must have found a way to keep walking, as that book is finished and out in the world. Some people think it is brilliant and a few people think it is awful – that's okay – that's not the point. The point is to not let the wobbles kick me off the path entirely. Regardless of what the finished book or project will look like, as Ibn Arabi said in one of my favourite quotes, "If you engage in travel, you will arrive."

When I had the thought 'it's just a wobble' earlier, I created a little space around the edges of the insecurity. Into this small space, an idea sneaked. Write about the wobble! I made myself a cup of chicory, hot and dark, and came back to my desk. I began this chapter, and kept walking...

Questions for reflection

When was your last wobble?

What shape do your wobbles tend to take? Crises of confidence? Hopelessness? Indulgence in compulsions? Leaving things unfinished or falling into blame?

What has helped you in the past with your wobbles?

What wobbles have you successfully negotiated? Did you learn anything on the journey?

Why do you need to keep walking? Why do you want to or choose to keep walking?

What helps you find your way back to the path?

What do you need to tell yourself right now?

Nature heals

> *The best remedy for those who are afraid, lonely or unhappy is to go outside, somewhere where they can be quite alone with the heavens, nature and God. Because only then does one feel that all is as it should be and that God wishes to see people happy, amidst the simple beauty of nature. As long as this exists, and it certainly always will, I know that then there will always be comfort for every sorrow, whatever the circumstances may be. And I firmly believe that nature brings solace in all troubles.*
> *~ Anne Frank*

I've just come inside from visiting the temple bunnies, Poppet and Peter. They are outside rabbits and they live in a cosy hutch which opens into an aviary, so they have lots of space to run around.

Since Peter and Poppet came to live with us, I've been more connected to the outside world. Their litter tray needs changing every day, whether it's raining or snowing. Their water bottle needs refilling regardless of how busy I am or what kind of mood I'm in. Most days we let them out into the top garden and sit with them awhile so they can nibble at the poor passion flowers and do binkies for the sheer joy of it.

Sliding open our glass doors and stepping from inside to outside never fails to have an effect on me. My lungs blossom and suck in the cool fresh air. My eyes perk up at all the new colours and shapes. The sky hangs above me, strewn with fluffy clouds or heavy and grey. I connect to the ground under my feet – this morning soggy and sticky, and sometimes baked hard by the sun. Nature takes my little body-and-mind with its small aches and worries and it puts it into relationship with *all that*.

How small we are, compared to that bank of cloud or to Bredon hill in the purple distance. How short the length of our life is, when we consider the lush yew tree in North Wales that is four thousand years old. How little we know.

Sometimes we need nature to infect us with wildness – we need unmanaged forests and craggy rocks with the sea crashing onto them. Sometimes we need the peace of soft grass and daisies, lying on our backs with the sun illuminating leaves and warming our cheeks. Sometimes we need to be reminded of how little we control, as we are asked to surrender to the erratic weather, turning our face to the wind. Whatever we need, nature will provide it, if we let her.

Nature heals. Go outside every day, even if only to look up at the sky for a few minutes before hurrying back inside. Let her bless you.

Questions for reflection

How often do you visit nature?

What are your favourite bits of the natural world?

What in nature makes you feel uncomfortable? What might you learn from these bits?

What happens when you walk in nature? Are you oblivious to it? What are you drawn to? What do you want to touch or smell?

How could you visit nature more often?

Can you spend a few minutes outside or looking out of a window right now?

Know yourself

> *We awaken to self-knowledge through the relentless practice of self-observation. Self-observation is not analysis; it is simply noticing what we think, how we think, what we fear, how we react, and what our strategies of behaviour are. Notice, notice, notice.* ~ Ezra Bayda

It is always possible to be surprised by people. We might assume that we know someone inside out after being their spouse or brother or friend for decades. We become confident that we can predict their behaviour or even that we know what they're thinking. Then they do something entirely unexpected, or we overhear them talking to someone else and we don't recognise them at all.

We don't like these holes in our knowledge. They make us feel unsafe. If we can't predict the behaviour of our best friend, then how can we trust anyone? We make ourselves feel safer in various ways. We might convince ourselves that we spotted the new behaviour coming and write it into the story we have about our friend. We might ignore what we witnessed, sometimes without even clocking it before it slides into unconsciousness. We might get angry or upset with the other person, or withdraw from the relationship without knowing why.

The same is true in our relationships with ourselves. Maybe we've always known ourselves as 'someone who copes', but a crisis stretches us to our limits and we begin to wonder if we can continue. Maybe we hold onto our identity as 'good husband' despite what our wife is telling us. As human beings we are uncomfortable with not-knowing, and there is nothing more unsettling than not knowing who we are. To deal with this uncertainty we construct elaborate and rigid stories about exactly who we are and what we're capable of. We started writing these stories when we were very young – 'when I cry too loud I am rejected', or 'to get the toy I want, I just have to use my strength'.

What stories do you tell yourself about who you are? The stories we are preoccupied with tend to be the ones we feel more insecure about, and so we tell them again and again to keep ourselves convinced. Our favourite stories might also be the ones we really rely on to prop ourselves up. We might find ourselves in the role of victim, telling other people how awful the world is and seeking their collusion, because this means we don't have to take responsibility. We might tell stories about the sacrifices we've made as a parent, as deep down we might fear that we're not doing a good enough job, or that we're selfish. These stories can become a defence – against facing the truth of our impermanent nature, and against acknowledging things about ourselves that we'd rather not know.

The downside of these cumbersome stories is that they obscure the delicate and ever-shifting truth about ourselves. They become like the stiff armour we put on to face the world, making us clumsy and less able to be responsive to what's actually happening. In reality, we are more complex than we could ever imagine. Consider the brain, with its one hundred billion cells. That's 100 000 000 000. These cells aren't just storing static memories or facts about 'who we are'. We are recreating ourselves all the time –reinterpreting old events as we have new experiences, forgetting things, healing small traumas and making new decisions.

One of the best ways I've found of getting to know myself is to use the Internal Family Systems model, where different parts of us (like the Always-Working-Hard part, the Critical part, or the Frightened Child part) are seen as independent 'entities' with lives of their own. As we identify these parts and get into conversation with them, we discover how complex each of them are, and how they are all in a web of relationships with each other just like members of a family. The model holds that all our parts, even the most troublesome, have positive intentions, and that we have the wisdom and compassion we need to work on any conflicted relationships between parts and reduce the polarisation that leads to dysfunction. It also holds that we shouldn't dive in and mess about with our most vulnerable, wounded parts until we've checked this out with the parts that have been protecting them for us (or protecting us from the intensity of their emotion). Using IFS methods, I've been gifted with access to some of these wounded parts of myself for the first time, and I've experienced a great deal of healing. If you're interested in exploring your own inner landscape in this way, I suggest you start with Self-Therapy by Jay Earley, read any of Richard C Schwartz's books, or find an IFS therapist to work with.

When you embark upon the lifelong project of knowing yourself, remember that you are bigger, more complicated and more fluid than you can ever imagine. Know that there will be things you don't want to know about yourself. They will be in hiding – you might only catch glimpses of them. Remember also that the whole business of re-evaluating who we think we are (and entering into the place of not-knowing) makes us feel wobbly. We need to approach ourselves gently, as if we want to become friends. We make friends with people when we are interested, patient and kind, and when we act in a way that helps them feel safe. The same is true of getting to know ourselves. We approach ourselves as if we were a shy stranger. We make a practice of noticing how we behave and what we think and we meet whatever we find with kindness, even the scaly, slimy creatures we glimpse from the corner of our eye.

Getting to know ourselves more intimately is helpful because it allows us to make choices based on a more accurate version of reality. We might notice that we have a strong story about 'not being able to cook' which is stopping us from experimenting in the kitchen, and decide to try out a new recipe for falafel anyway. We might notice that we often make jokes when our friends ask us how we are, and experiment with being more honest with them instead. Whether or not we make different choices, getting to know new parts of ourselves can be transformative in itself. Pause right now and tune into your shoulders – notice how they are feeling, and where there are any tight spots or tension. Don't try and change them, just notice exactly where the tightness is. If you're like me, your muscles will start to release all by themselves. The kind of self-observation that Ezra Bayda is talking about will inexorably lead to change.

Self-knowledge is also precious because it helps us to guess what it's like to be someone else. Unless we can make this leap of imagination we won't find our way to empathy – to feeling a warm affinity with others because we have some sense of what it's like to be them. As limited, embodied beings we have a lot in common when you get down to the basics – we are all afraid, and we all want to be seen and appreciated. The more we know about the different parts of ourselves, the more we will be able to identify and empathise with a full range of experiences in others. As Eleanor Wilner said, "The further inside one goes, the more one finds everybody."

I'm hoping that as you get to know yourself you will also grow fonder of yourself, as you do your oldest friends. You don't just love your friends despite their fallibilities, but because of them. You know that behind each annoying habit or prickly defence is a tender spot, aching for love. As we get closer to those bits of ourselves that we find distasteful or even abhorrent, we just keep going. Noticing, noticing, noticing, and welcoming it all in, just as it is.

Questions for reflection

Who are you?

Which parts of yourself are you pleased by?

Which parts of yourself are you disappointed by or ashamed of?

What might their positive intention be?

What activities contribute to your self-knowledge? Do you journal, or talk with friends about what you've noticed about yourself?

What are you afraid of finding?

What are your favourite stories about yourself? Do these help you or hinder you?

What do your friends say about you?

What do your critics say about you?

What have you noticed about yourself recently? How can you continue to get to know these parts of yourself?

How can you become more friendly towards yourself? How could you be more kind?

Peaks and troughs

> *To every thing there is a season, and a time to every purpose under the heaven: A time to be born, and a time to die; a time to plant, and a time to pluck up that which is planted...* ~ Ecclesiastes 3

The first job I got after University was working in the Call Centre of a financial services company. We took many dozens of calls a day from people wanting to know how much their bond was worth or wanting to change their address. I had aspirations to join the team of glamorous Call Centre Coaches, who were the guardians of excellent customer service. They seemed to Know Things about people and about helping others, and they floated around the Call Centre with a self-possessed air I was desperate to emulate.

In time I did make it into the team, and I started to soak up the wisdom they possessed. They had their own way of doing things and their own language. One of the phrases they used was 'peaks and troughs' as a way of describing how everything we do can be plotted as a wavy graph. Sometimes we work intensely, and sometimes less intensely. Sometimes we feel confident, and sometimes insecure. They tended to use it when we had an occasional long lunch at a local Italian, as a jokey way of excusing themselves from guilt, but it has stayed with me and I still keep it in my pocket, a shiny pebble of wisdom.

I find it especially helpful because I am prone to workaholism. The part of my brain that is addled by 'ought' is convinced that I should have only one mode – productive. As long as I'm getting things done, I feel okay. The problem is that no human being can continue to be productive ad infinitum. They will have periods of high energy and focus, when they plough through their to do list, and they will have hours or days or even weeks of low energy, when they need to rest, reflect and recuperate. Peaks and troughs.

I need to remind myself that I am allowed troughs as well as peaks. If there weren't any troughs, there wouldn't be any peaks. In Spring it is the time to plant, and in Autumn it is time to harvest. Troughs aren't just wasted time. When we leave a field to rest for a season, we are giving the soil a chance to replenish itself, to replace the sucked-up nutrients. When I'm not productive it not only gives my body and brain a chance to rest, but it allows thoughts and feelings to 'compost' and give rise to fresh green shoots.

Your peaks and troughs might be different from mine. Maybe you need to remember that, in order to continue giving to others, you need to have times when you are receiving from others. Maybe you need to spend as well as to save, or the other way around. Maybe you need to remember a time in your life when you did feel more capable or happier, and trust that you'll get there again.

We might want to smooth our peaks and troughs out a little, especially if they are particularly jagged. We can do this by paying attention to what tips us into one mode or another, and deciding what medicine we need – maybe more support and feedback from colleagues if we swing wildly from insecurity to over-confidence, or a savings plan if we careen from famine to feast. If you tend towards always being super-disciplined or ultra-slobby, you might want to move your wavy line a little further up or down.

It's good to aim for the middle way, but it isn't realistic to expect that we will ever flatten the line completely. Sometimes we will be fatter, and sometimes thinner. Sometimes we'll be able to work efficiently, sometimes less so. Be kind to yourself when you're up, and be kind to yourself when you're down. Follow the wisdom of the Call Centre coaches. Peaks and troughs.

Questions for reflection

In what areas of your life do you expect yourself to always be doing well?

What would a 'trough' look like in this area of your life?

How might experiencing a 'trough' be helpful for you? What judgements come up when I ask this question?

What do you say to yourself when you are in troughs? How kind are you?

Are there any areas of your life where you spend too much time in troughs and not enough in peaks? How might you help yourself to spend more time in peaks?

In what areas of your life would you like to move the wavy line up a bit or down a bit?

Can you feel the relief of the unavoidable reality of peaks and troughs?

Detach with love

You cannot save people. You can only love them.
~ Anaïs Nin

When someone we care about is suffering, we also suffer. It's hard to witness a human being in pain, and even harder when that human being is someone we love very much.

The people who attend Al-Anon, a 12 Step group for those affected by someone else's drinking, are experts in this sort of suffering. They have watched their sons drink themselves out of three good jobs and a marriage, or they have grown up concealing the truth for an alcoholic parent. They have witnessed their spouse in anguish as their health declines and they continue to drink.

When people first join Al-Anon, they are desperate to find out how they can control the other person's drinking. They've already tried all sorts of things by the time they come to the group – pleading, hiding alcohol, making threats, getting other people involved, punishing, controlling and manipulation – and the alcoholic has continued to drink. Surely Al-Anon must have the answer?

As they sit and listen to the stories of those who've been in the group for a while, they begin to hear that they didn't cause the drinking, they can't control it, and they can't cure it. They are advised to detach with love (DETACH – Don't Ever

Think About Changing Him/Her). They hear how others began to have a healthier relationship with their alcoholic others, and started to take responsibility for their own lives. They begin to realise that they have had their own part to play in the alcoholic situation. They have colluded with the alcoholic, or rescued them when their drinking got them into trouble. They have become entangled in matters that are none of their business. Some admit to feeling a sense of superiority, or of finding comfort in knowing that they are doing better than their alcoholic other. As they become clearer about their own codependency, they begin to heal. As time goes on they discover a hope that they never imagined possible – that they can find happiness whether the alcoholic is drinking or not.

You may or may not identify with being troubled by someone else's drinking, but we have all been disturbed by the compulsive, destructive or inappropriate behaviour of someone close to us. In my own experience this disturbed feeling comes from two sources – one is a feeling of empathy and compassion for them in their suffering, and the other is a fear that we won't be okay if the other person continues to do what they're doing. This fear pushes us to becoming subtly (or not so subtly!) invested in the other person being a particular way for our benefit, not for theirs.

This fear can be huge, and for good reason. We might dread our husband leaving us as we rely on his income, and so we put up with his physical abuse as a 'necessary cost' of feeding ourselves and our children. We may depend on our partner for her affirmation of us, and so we ignore her affairs because the alternative would be being alone and unloved. We expend enormous energy attempting to change the other person, or we pretend that we feel okay about what is happening.

We are all driven by this fear in our relationships sometimes, and most of the time it doesn't lead to any lasting problems. We cook our wife a nice meal before asking about going away on a weekend trip with a friend, or we exaggerate our illness when we want to be looked after. We start getting into trouble when we lose touch with our own basic sense of being-okay and rely completely on the other person to make us okay, or the opposite – when we think that the other person will only be okay if we are directing them. We make the other person into our Higher Power, or we decide that we are their Higher Power.

What if we're convinced that the other person would do better in their life if only they'd listen to us? Well, if it was that easy, they'd already be listening. It's impossible to judge how difficult it is for another person to make different choices – if their wounds are deep then their defences may be almost impenetrable. It can help us to remember what it's like for us when we're in the deepest forests of our own compulsions or dark thoughts – it can feel practically impossible to find our way back to the light, even if someone is yelling at us that we should just turn left at the next tree.

How much of a choice the other person has in their suffering is irrelevant anyway – we cannot live their life for them. This is the most difficult part of receiving wisdom from Al-Anon. New members slowly realise that the only person they can change is themselves. These movements towards health in their own life – setting appropriate boundaries, becoming less dependent on the alcoholic, engaging in self-care – may contribute to the alcoholic moving towards their own health, and they may not.

As we live our own life in wholesome recovery, taking responsibility for ourselves and finding wisdom and serenity, some people will witness us changing and will be inspired to turn towards their own recovery. But we can't make this happen. In the rooms (the tatty community spaces or cold churches – the sacred spaces – where various 12 Step meetings take place) it is said that an alcoholic is like a person in deep water who is afraid of swimming. The water is rising. Standing around him or her are various people who hold them up – the spouse who hides the extent of the problem from their friends, the understanding work supervisor who puts up with the absences, the friend who doesn't mention all the money she's lent. If we continue to collude with the illness, protecting them from the worst of the consequences, then the person can continue drinking – not happily, because being in the grips of addiction is a hellish place to be – but not going under.

When we detach with love, we step away from the alcoholic or whoever it is who is making (in our view) bad choices, and we let them get thoroughly wet. This moment is an opportunity – the person might feel themselves beginning to drown and seek some help. They may also beckon someone else over to take our place and keep them out of the water. We have no control over whether they will take the opportunity or not. Indeed, it isn't our business. Whether or not they are able to make the healthy choice, we make the healthy choice for ourselves, by not standing there forever. We continue to love them, and we also get on with our own lives.

This is a harsh message. I know – I spent years watching someone I loved slowly killing themselves. I wish it were otherwise. The serenity prayer reminds us that we need wisdom to know the difference between the things we can change (ourselves) and the things we can't (other people). We abandon the project of saving our 'other', by realising that we could never keep them afloat in the first place. We hand the other person back to their Higher Power with love. The only person we can save is ourselves. When we are saved, we light the way for others.

Questions for reflection

When do you get tangled up in other people's problems?

Who do you depend on to be a particular way? What happens when they don't do what you want them to do?

Is it helpful for them when you rescue them or when you suffer terribly as a result of their suffering?

How might you detach with love?

What do you think would happen if you detached with love? What is the worse case scenario? How would you survive that?

What happens when you do detach? What feelings come up? Guilt? Fear? A sense of helplessness?

How good are you at setting appropriate boundaries with other people? Do you know what appropriate boundaries are?

Do you need to seek specialist help (a group, some therapy) to deal with any issues that have arisen for you as you've read this chapter?

Is there someone you admire who is able to detach with love? How do they do it?

Are you ready to save yourself?

Bow often

> *A desire to kneel down sometimes pulses through my body, or rather it is as if my body has been meant and made for the act of kneeling. Sometimes, in moments of deep gratitude, kneeling down becomes an overwhelming urge, head deeply bowed, hands before my face.* ~ Etty Hillesum

We do a lot of bowing in my Amida Shu Buddhist tradition. We bow when we enter the shrine room, and we bow to our seats before we sit down. We bow with the voice of the singing bowl at the beginning of meditation and at the end. We prostrate before the Buddha five times to a melodious chant - Namo Amida Bu, Namo Amida Bu - laying our chests flat onto the floor and lifting our hands above our heads.

When we shape our body into particular positions, our minds, emotions and spirit follow. When we are feeling low and we straighten our back and lift our chin, we may feel a little upsurge of confidence. If you force your face into the shape of a smile right now, you may feel a slight glow of warmth, radiating from around your eyes. Bowing, whether a bend at the waist or a dip of our heads with our hands in anjali, or putting the whole length of our bodies on the floor, also leads to a change in attitude.

Bowing is generally seen as a way of paying respect to someone or something that is more worthy of respect than we are – we are putting them above us. This sentence may raise your hackles! In the West we don't like to think of ourselves as 'less than' others, feeling that this will be bad for our self-esteem or that we're giving the other person permission to see us as inferior or to treat us badly. We feel that we would be abasing ourselves. This misses the true spirit of bowing.

When I bow, I am saying thank you for what I have received. I bow to my meditation cushion after service to say thank you for supporting me – not just to the cushion, but to whoever it was that wove the purple material, to whoever stitched it, to the sun for growing the dried buckwheat that fills it. When I bow to the shrine I am saying thank you to the Buddha for the teachings he gave two and a half thousand years ago. When I bow to my fellow congregants after service I am saying thank you to them for sharing practice with me.

Of course, sometimes we bow whether we feel grateful or not. We offer our elders respect in recognition of their experience, and we offer the same to anyone who has travelled the path for longer than we have, whether the path is a career, a spiritual path or a group. We can pay respect to people in this way regardless of whether we always agree with them. Nobody (except the Buddha!) is perfect, but this doesn't stop us from seeing the wisdom in them and bowing to this. We bow to the fragments of Buddha within each person, and we stay open to learning from them.

Zen master Suzuki Shunryu said: "A master who cannot bow to his disciple cannot bow to Buddha. Sometimes the master and disciple bow together to Buddha. Sometimes we may bow to cats and dogs..." I learn so much from my psychotherapy clients and my Buddhist students – that is a good reason to bow to them. I receive so much from our three cats – purrs, patience, the simple pleasure of their presence – that is a good reason to bow to them. What reasons can you find to bow to your children, to your friends, and to the garden? What about the woman at the supermarket check-out, your painful back, or your grumpy neighbour? Can we bow to everything?

When I bow it reminds me of my own fallibility and of the deeply contingent nature of my continued existence. I am dependent on so many things and so many people for my survival. I can forget this when I'm standing upright, directing things, and complaining about what I haven't got.

The other thing I love about bowing and especially prostrations is that, once I'm down on the floor, I can surrender. I can let go of needing to be in charge of everything, and I have a tangible experience of being supported. The floor supports me and I just melt into it. The Buddha is there, watching over me. The back of my neck is exposed to my enemies, but I trust that I will be okay and rest completely in the moment. Even as I type these words I notice myself releasing a long out-breath, and feel the muscles in my neck and shoulders relaxing. We can surrender, and we can trust.

When I connect with my vulnerability in this way, I feel that I become stronger, not weaker. I am not abasing myself but being honest about the paltry nature of what I offer compared to what I receive, and at the tininess of my wisdom compared to the wisdom of the world. I come from a place of humble realism rather than a puffed-up bossiness, and there is a real power in this. We don't bow because we want to get more power – that wouldn't work! – but we surprise ourselves by finding a quiet strength within us when we are truly at peace with giving it away.

Bowing keeps us supple and graceful. It keeps us humble and grateful. Bow to everything and everyone you meet today. I'm bowing to you right now. _/_

Questions for reflection

What do the words humility and contrition conjure for you?

Is there anyone you admire who you would characterise as humble? How does this affect how they live their lives?

When are you less likely to be humble? When do you get puffed-up?

Who or what is it easy to bow to?

Who or what is more difficult to bow to?

When you next find someone difficult, experiment with bowing to the wisdom and love in them in your mind. What happens?

You might want to experiment with doing five prostrations and kneeling or lying on the floor. You can do your prostrations in front of something beautiful, a person in your mind, the sun, or anything. How does it feel to put yourself so low to the ground? Can you relax?

Would you like to incorporate a bow into your daily practice?

Ask for help

Help only comes to those who ask for it.
~ J. K. Rowling

Put your hand up if you're excellent at asking for help.

I thought so. Most of us struggle with this. I certainly haven't got my hand up. I am excellent at the opposite – struggling on, taking responsibility for more than is appropriate, and pushing my body and mind until they begin to fray. I am not so good at stopping and simply saying 'would somebody be willing to help me with this, please?'

Asking for help is hard because it makes us vulnerable. In the act of revealing our limits, we are showing someone our soft underbelly. We don't know whether they will stroke us gently or tickle us, hurt us or ignore us.

Asking for help is hard because it puts us in touch with our inherent fallibility – the precarious nature of our self-reliance. What would it take to sweep aside our carefully constructed self-sufficiency – a fall, a serious illness, a minor financial disaster? Most of the things that disrupt our plans are beyond our control. We avoid acknowledging the extent to which our continued safety is contingent on external events, but these things could happen. Something like this *will* happen, sooner or later.

Our experience of our vulnerability when we admit to needing help is precisely what opens us up to the greatest gifts. It gives us an opportunity to practice trusting, as we take a leap of faith and ask another person or the Universe to take care of us. It helps us to get to know ourselves better, including the tender parts of ourselves that need healing or attention. It also connects us to the same vulnerability in everyone else. It's much easier to find compassion for people in their fallibility and dependence when we have had a recent experience of our own.

Asking for help also gives someone else an opportunity to help us. This is a highly underrated positive side effect of asking for help. When we ask for help, we are saying to someone that we trust them to see our limitations. We are also trusting them to make the right decision about whether or not to say yes to our request. Worrying that other people will say yes and then resent helping me is a big obstacle to my asking for help. This is partly because I sometimes still struggle to say no to requests when I should, and then project this onto other people, and partly because I fear that people won't put up with much inconvenience from me.

Despite my fears, I know that people are usually glad to be asked for help and then given an opportunity to provide that help. It makes us feel good to be of use to others, and we can also take pleasure in seeing our help gratefully received. One of the most ingenious parts of the Alcoholics Anonymous programme is that newly sobered up alcoholics are encouraged to help others and offer service in their group very early on, even if it's just making the tea. This is crucial in beginning to rebuild self-esteem and reminds the person that, despite sometimes overwhelming evidence to the contrary, they are capable of helping other people in their own recovery and of being valuable members of society.

Learning to ask for help and learning how to respond to requests for help is an art, and like any art we become more skilful as we keep practising. We will all have our own strengths and our areas for improvement. One of my biggest learning edges is how to ask for help more directly.

I am an expert hinter. Hinting is much safer than being direct. I don't expose myself to the possibility of being refused, or reveal my vulnerability. I remember walking in London with my sister-in-law many years ago, and making various casual comments about how fast she was walking, how unfit I was, how it was good for me to get some exercise – hint hint hint. Eventually she turned round, slightly frustrated, and asked me if I wanted her to slow down. Even then, it was too hard for me to admit it – to say yes, I am struggling to keep up with you, please could you slow down a bit. I didn't want to be an inconvenience, and I was embarrassed that my fitness levels were so poor.

Sometimes people will give us what we need when we drop hints, or manipulate them, or guilt them or become martyrs. But it doesn't feel good for them, and it doesn't feel good for us. It's not a 'clean' transaction. When I ask for help in roundabout ways I often feel frustrated that the other person doesn't seem to get what I'm saying (because I'm not being clear!). The person I'm asking can feel confused by mixed messages, that they're getting it wrong, or feel pressured into capitulating to the request. Both the person asking and the person giving are missing out on an opportunity to connect more authentically.

If we are able to admit to ourselves and to the Universe that we are in need of something, in my experience we are much more likely to get it. I wrote to a friend recently as I was worried that he was siding with a mutual colleague in an argument and withdrawing their support from me as a result. The first two emails I wrote were confusing and, as I made no request and my colleague was probably a bit confused by them, I received no response. Only on my third attempt did I admit directly to my feelings of vulnerability, and my need to know whether this person was able to support me as well as my colleague. He wrote back immediately with surprise that I would feel that way and with reassurances. I felt I'd made myself perfectly clear in the previous two emails, but apparently not! If you are interested in learning more about how to ask for what you need more directly, and without blaming the other (which allows the other to choose to give more freely), I'd recommend Nonviolent Communication by Marshall Rosenburg.

Asking for help can open us up to good things that would never have happened otherwise. We might get to know someone new, or receive something unexpected and wonderful. We might get some practice at feeling 'worthy'. We might offer reassurance to someone who has always seen us as invulnerable and who is relieved to see that we're human too!

Of course, there are never any guarantees. An important part of practising to ask for help is learning that our wishes won't always be granted, and in some cases we may even be exploited. In her excellent book 'The Art of Asking', Amanda Palmer writes about how her fans have very occasionally disrespected her when she's made herself vulnerable by trusting them and asking them for things throughout her career. When we expose our soft underbelly, every so often someone will tickle us or even hurt us. This is how it is to be in the world with an open heart.

Sometimes we just write these experiences off as unlucky. In our first few months of running the temple, someone stole money from a handbag in the temple hallway. There was some pressure at the time to get a security camera installed, but instead we made sure we tightened up on locking the front door and then carried on as before – more than three years later there have been no further issues. Sometimes we need to get wiser about who we make ourselves vulnerable to, or when. It took me many years to realise that whenever I turned to a particular friend when I was feeling wobbly, she immediately started worrying about me and I ended up reassuring her. Eventually I started taking my wobbly feelings to different friends. This discrimination process is also an art, and we need to find a middle way between being over-trusting and being over-defended. As it says in Codependents Anonymous literature, we gradually 'learn to trust those who are trustworthy'.

How do we handle those people who ask for help too often? Maybe you have a friend who is always borrowing money and then 'forgetting' to give it back, or a colleague who expects you to bail them out when they repeatedly fail to meet their deadlines. Or what do we do when someone asks us for something perfectly reasonable but we just don't have the capacity to meet their need?

What is helpful here is to learn the art of acknowledging our limits and setting appropriate boundaries. If we don't currently have the energy to take another crisis call from our friend, we can let them know – kindly and with a suggestion that they call back later or try someone else. If we feel our colleague is avoiding facing their issues with time management, we can be honest about our uncomfortable feelings about bailing them out, or describe how it interrupts our own work and ask if there's a different way we could help.

Asking for and receiving help needs to feel good for both people, like a kiss. Of course sometimes our help is needed as the result of a crisis, and regardless of our capacity we just have to get on with doing what needs to be done, but usually when we are asked there is an option to offer something different, or at a different time. If we respond to someone's request though a feeling of 'ought', resentment will follow like slime from a snail. Some of these feelings will leak out into our actions, however well we think we are disguising them.

The help-asker will find it easier to trust you in the future if you can give them a gentle but honest response. It will also help you to trust yourself – to know that you will offer only what feels possible and good, and that you won't allow yourself to become overwhelmed by other's needs. If we can keep checking in with ourselves in this way, and as we become more grounded over time, we often find that our capacity for offering help grows.

Offer someone else an opportunity to help, and create an opening so you can receive. Yes, it might be difficult. It opens us up to the horrible risk of being rejected or ignored or exploited or judged. We are like hermit crabs stepping outside of our shells.

It's worth learning how. Try it today. Start small, with someone you trust. Remind yourself that if you get a 'no', you will survive. When we step outside of our shells, we are inviting the sun to shine on our bare skin. The sun is love.

Questions for reflection

How often do you ask for help?

How do you feel when you ask?

What stops you from asking for help? What are you most worried about?

Who do you ask for help? Who don't you ask? Why is this?

What happens when you do ask for help?

How do you feel when the person helping doesn't do whatever you've asked them to do in the same way you would?

What happens when others ask you for help? Do you project this experience onto others when asking them?

What do you need help with in your life right now? Who could you ask?

Do you ever ask for help as a way of avoiding something you haven't taken responsibility for or faced?

What are your strengths and weaknesses in the art of asking for help and responding to requests for help? Do you understand why you have these strengths and weaknesses?

When can you next practice asking for help?

Chuck should

> *Everything is something you decide to do, and there is nothing you have to do.* ~ Denis Waitley

From the moment we are born, pink, wrinkled and raw, the world assaults us with its 'shoulds'. Come over here, now here, be weighed, drink this, now carefully watch the ones who look after you and pay attention to who they need you to be. We internalise a myriad of 'shoulds' and 'oughts' in an attempt to stay acceptable and they lie deep in our psyches like unexploded land mines.

These 'shoulds' accompany us as we grow, and multiply. We should be thinner, richer, kinder and funnier, with glossier hair. Other people should stop letting us down and give us better presents. The world should make things easier for us.

We all have our own particular constellation of 'shoulds'. One of my biggest is that I should be doing more – more work, more gardening, faster personal growth, faster spiritual progress, more writing.

'Should' is a perniciously unhelpful word. It helps us to pretend that we have no choice in the things we are doing. When I feel that I should be working rather than drinking tea with my friend on a Tuesday afternoon, what I mean is that my programming has a strong preference that I continue working, and that it would feel uncomfortable to resist it. Whether I choose to continue drinking tea or drag myself back to work is entirely up to me.

My suggestion is that you stop saying 'should' and instead say 'choose to' or 'would like to' instead. This leads us towards honesty and helps us to see what is actually happening. We can decide that we would like to make our children a healthy tea when we get home from a very long day, even though we are exhausted, because we value their well-being. We can say that our body would probably appreciate getting more exercise, but it isn't our priority to go to the gym at the moment. We can say that we choose to work at a soul-crushing job because we value our family's security over the risk of leaving without having somewhere else to go. Some of the choices available to us aren't great ones, but if we can remember that we are always choosing it will transform us from passive victims into active players in our lives.

I find it helpful to be very gentle with myself around my strongest programming. Our compulsions and habits think that they are getting us what we need or even keeping us alive, and so they will do whatever is necessary to make us go back to work rather than drink the cup of tea. This programming is wily and insidious. To help us move away from the feeling of 'should', we can practice knowing ourselves, asking for help, radical honesty, taking refuge, and anything that begins to ground us in faith. This will begin to neutralise the fear that drives the behaviour.

One of the most powerful antidotes I have to my shoulds around work is the quote from the Bible where we are told that we won't have to become workaholics to be good students: "Take my yoke upon you and learn from me, for I am gentle and humble in heart, and you will find rest for your souls. For my yoke is easy and my burden is light." (Matthew 11:29-30). Letting go of 'shoulds' and 'oughts' can be a great relief like this. You can wholeheartedly embrace having a disgustingly filthy car until the time comes when you choose to clear it out. You don't clean it because you should, and you also don't waste energy feeling guilty about something you're choosing. Yes, you might prefer to have it clean, and yes you might worry about people judging you, but evidently not enough to get out the buckets. You're the kind of person who lets their car get filthy – so there it is. My Buddhist teacher says that his own teacher Rev. Jiyu Kennett advised that if you were going to sin you should 'sin vigorously'. The idea is that if we approach our sinning wholeheartedly, getting honest with ourselves and taking our behaviour as far as it wants to go, that we are more likely to discover the downside more quickly. After wholeheartedly entering into eating quantities of chocolate, we might feel more like avoiding chocolate for a long time.

Look at what shape your body is in, check your bank balance, and look at the state of your kitchen or your desk. Reflect on your current behaviour. Look at your work, your leisure time, and your relationships. This is what is. This is what you are currently choosing. If you would like to change some things, then fine – begin to make changes. If change feels impossible, be clear about your intention, keep shining love on yourself, and change will probably ensue when the time is ripe. Otherwise you can simply acknowledge that you're choosing not to make changes right now. Look at me, with my filthy car and my overgrown garden, drinking tea on a work day with a friend. This is who I am, and that's okay!

Questions for reflection

How many 'shoulds' and 'oughts' are there in your life?

When are the 'shoulds' most strong?

Where are you most resistant to seeing your 'shoulds' as a choice you're making? Why do you think that is?

Are your 'shoulds' ever helpful?

How is it to change a few of your 'shoulds' to 'choose to'?

How would it be to know that you are deciding not to prioritise doing more exercise, cleaning the car etc. right now, and be okay with that?

Monitor your speech or thoughts over the next few days and see how many 'shoulds' and 'oughts' pop up. See if you can replace them.

Be heard

> *...when a person realizes he has been deeply heard, his eyes moisten. I think in some real sense he is weeping for joy. It is as though he were saying, "Thank God, somebody heard me. Someone knows what it's like to be me." ~ Carl Rogers*

It is a rare thing to be truly heard. We have a spiritual practice called a 'listening circle', where we take turns to hold a stone and speak while everyone else is quiet and listens. People are often overwhelmed when they first take the stone; at all the attention focussed on them, at the promise that nobody will interrupt or give their opinion. It's almost too much. People often share things they never expected to, or end up wiping tears from their cheeks.

If they come back a few times, they begin to appreciate their time with the stone. They receive it as a gift and hold it quietly, absorbing the warmth of other people's hands. They wonder about what is current for them. They allow pauses as they speak. Sometimes they allow emotion to accompany their words. They begin to see this time that they have with the stone as a precious thing.

The listening circle is a rich and fruitful place, as it teaches us to listen as well as giving us practice of being heard. We learn to listen to others without jumping to conclusions, and we keep an open mind about the person we're listening to. We learn much about ourselves as we listen to other people struggling with similar issues. We see our own reflection in other people. As we hear someone sharing their shame or vulnerability, fellow feeling wells up in us naturally.

When someone shows me with their body or their voice that they have heard me, I am relieved and grateful. In order to do this, they have to care about me – even if it's just a little bit, or just in that moment. They have to bring their attention away from themselves and place it on me, feeling curious about how it is to be me, asking questions or checking that they have understood. When I'm heard, I feel relieved that someone else is there with me and that they can understand my inner language – maybe not every word, but enough to translate it into their own inner language. I am no longer alone in a strange land.

Being heard can also leave us feeling vulnerable. It may be that, as we speak, we discover new things about ourselves that we'd rather not have known. We may feel shame as we admit these things to another person, and fear about how they might judge us. This is especially true if we have had experiences of being judged when we were growing up. We might even worry that our listener will use our words against us, now they know where our tender spots are.

Listening and being heard lead us towards intimacy, and intimacy can be a scary place. Of course, it's also where the good stuff happens! It's important to be kind to ourselves as we practice opening up. We can choose our listeners carefully, and we can acknowledge our fears. We can share our fears with our listeners, stop speaking whenever we want to, and take things as slowly as we need to. Being listened to is an art and, just like any other, it takes practice.

If being heard is a rare thing, how can we arrange more opportunities where it might happen? There are many sacred spaces where it is more likely that you will be heard. These include all the 12 Step groups, support groups and other structured groups. You could decide to work with a therapist or a coach. You might ask to speak to your religious leader or an older trusted family member or colleague. If you are distressed or lonely you could call the Samaritans or other helplines. The people in these spaces will be human, and so not all of them will be skilled at listening. We need to feel safe before we share from our hearts – be patient, trust your instincts, and if you have concerns, raise them or look for somewhere or someone different.

We can also start to gently educate our friends about good listening. We can model good listening by paying proper attention to them – by not interrupting, and by checking our understanding by reflecting back what they are saying in our own words. We can be specific about what we want from people before we begin: 'You might want to give me advice about this, but I'd really just like to get it off my chest – are you willing to just listen and let me know you've understood?'. We can let them know when we don't feel listened to – 'You seem distracted – would you rather I told you about this another time?' We can also express our gratitude when we do feel heard.

Regardless of how often others listen to us, we can always listen to ourselves. This sounds easier than it is. We are prone to all the same bad habits with ourselves as we are with other people. We might judge ourselves, or ignore ourselves, or jump to solutions before we've really understood exactly what's going on for us. We might also be impatient with ourselves when we don't really know how we feel.

When we're confused about what we're feeling, it can help to pause and really tune in to what's happening in our bodies. Is there tension in my stomach or neck? How is my breathing? We can then ask ourselves a few questions – is there frustration in me? What happened today that might have upset me? Ask the same questions you would ask a friend, and pay yourself the same kind and patient attention. It may be that you just sit quietly for a while with the part of yourself that is feeling something, putting an imaginary arm around it so it knows it isn't alone.

Once we've taken the time to hear ourselves properly, we will naturally become more interested in the world again. Listening to ourselves is described in Nonviolent Communication as self-empathy, and it is suggested that in situations of conflict it's only after we feel heard that we experience an internal shift and become interested in the other person again. We feel soothed or settled, and from this place we start to wonder what was going on for the other person when they spoke harshly to us or denied us something we've wanted. We can't rush self-empathy – if strong emotion has been stirred up we might need to keep listening patiently to ourselves for weeks or even longer before we take any action.

You can also always feel heard by the Universe or your Higher Power. A practice we sometimes use in Amida Shu is writing letters to Amida Buddha. I have a special golden notebook for this and when I want to be listened to, I write in this rather than in my usual journal. I start with 'Dear Amida', and then I say whatever it is I need to say. I'll share something I've been struggling with, or speak of an area of confusion, or maybe I'll ask for help. When I write in my golden notebook I feel more held and heard, and this brings me comfort.

In the realm of human relationship, quality is more important than quantity. A moment of really being heard and understood can connect us with a kind of infinite space, and be more valuable than several hours of airtime when we're not really connecting with the other. When we do feel heard, the person who is listening to us will often experience this as a gift. There is a sense of mutuality. We enter into a dance where, whoever happens to be leading, both dancers feel held by each other and by the ocean of light.

Questions for reflection

How often are you truly heard during your usual daily life?

Who in your life is better at listening?

Who in your life struggles to listen well? Why do you think this might be?

How well do you listen? What are your bad listening habits?

What new spaces could you find where you could be listened to?

What feelings come up when you feel heard? Do you feel unworthy or exposed? Grateful or relieved? What else?

Would you like to experiment with writing letters to the Universe or your Higher Power?

How often do you listen to yourself? How well do you listen to yourself?

What would you like to say right now, and have heard?

Change your conditions

> *We live in a world of objects. People, places and things are significant in our lives. They affect our moods, our thoughts and our expectations. When we see a rose flowering, we probably feel happy. When we hear a baby crying, we may feel upset or irritated. When we see a sunset we may feel inspired. When we see a good friend we may feel love.* ~ Caroline Brazier

All things are dependent on causes and conditions. This is one of the core Buddhist teachings – the theory of dependent origination. This theory is not deterministic – particular conditions will not lead to particular outcomes as a matter of certainty – but they will result in a greater likelihood of something particular happening. Our mental state is also dependent on causes and conditions, and so one of the most powerful ways we can influence our feelings and our behaviour is to change our conditions.

We can all relate to how this works in practice. This morning I didn't feel like doing my usual yoga. I did it anyway, and afterwards my body felt lighter and straighter. I spent some time with a friend who is steeped in sadness, and came away with a melancholy of my own which took some time to shake off. Soon I will get up from my desk and have a break outside, where I will stand under the empty blue sky, gaze at the view across the valley and feel my heart expand.

We are prone to underestimate the influence our conditions have over us, because we like to see ourselves as self-determining. We don't see ourselves as susceptible to adverts – others are. We're not influenced by peer pressure. We got good grades at school because of our own efforts, rather than mostly a lucky mix of genetics, family history and our date of birth.

When I was at University I went along to what was billed as an auction with a number of my intelligent, independent-minded friends. A charismatic salesman took the stage and started to work the crowd. I sat on a table right at the back where I switched from participant to observer. First of all, at least half the crowd were persuaded to part with a relatively small amount of money in return for a special ticket. Now they felt obligated to stay and listen to the man's smooth patter or they'd lose their money – they were hooked. I spotted a couple of 'plants' who were the first to hand over their money, and who would respond the most enthusiastically when the salesman stirred the crowd. They were slick! By the end of the lengthy sales process, most of the audience had spent money on things they didn't want or need. I can still remember my friend trying to justify spending £50 on a 'mystery item' in a silver briefcase which turned out to be a substandard camera with missing pieces. He was ashamed and in shock – we walked back home in silence and we never mentioned it again.

Acknowledging how powerfully we can be influenced by our conditions can help us to have empathy for ourselves and empathy for others. At the time of the sale I admit that I felt some scorn towards my University friends. How could they be so gullible as to be taken in? I realise now that this was a way of distancing myself from my own gullibility, and my own vulnerability to being conned. Whenever I start falling into this 'it would never happen to me' trap, I remind myself of a time when I was a young adult and travelled to college on the bus. One morning I sat next to a young teenager with learning disabilities and he started to masturbate. I'd seen him do it once or twice before and I'd been amazed that the people sitting next to him hadn't said or done anything, or at least moved seats. Here I was, sitting right there and pretending that nothing was happening. The power of social convention, the fear of 'making a scene' or drawing attention to myself, froze me into my seat. A few weeks later he sat next to a young schoolgirl with beautiful long blond hair and he did it again. Just like everyone else on the full bus, I did nothing.

We can never really know how we would act if we were in the place of another. If we'd experienced the terrible abuse that person had experienced, would we have avoided prison? If we'd been brought up by our colleague's parents, might we also resort to bullying as a way of keeping ourselves safe? If I'd handed over my money for a 'special ticket', would I have been the one stuck with the faulty camera?

If our conditions can be so powerful, then how much control or free will do we have when it comes to making different choices? I choose to think that we do always have a choice – even if there's only a miniscule crack of light. It might be almost impossible for an addict to decide to go into treatment, but there will be a moment or a series of moments when they choose which way to turn – towards the light or further away from it. This is true for me too. I'd love to say that

I stayed up too late last night watching television on my laptop because I was in the vice-like grip of an uncontrollable compulsion – it wasn't my fault! I did make a choice to click onto the next programme and then the next, however, regardless of how conditioned that choice was.

For me, this way of seeing the world – radical responsibility paired with an understanding of how massively difficult it can be to make a difference choice – gives me two things: hope that I and others can change, and empathy for myself and others when we just can't manage it. Sometimes we need to remind ourselves of the hope, and sometimes we need to reconnect with the empathy.

What sorts of things can we do to change our conditions? The first step is beginning to notice how and when we are being influenced. We can notice how we feel after seeing certain friends, or doing a particular class or activity. We can tune into our bodies. We can pay attention when we behave in a way that arouses our suspicion – 'I don't usually do that, why have I done it this time?'. This noticing takes decades! At the age of 42 I'm only just beginning to see how I abandon myself when I'm in a conflict, offering all my attention to the other rather than remaining present with my own feelings, needs and wisdom. Conditions tend to exert a much more powerful influence when they are doing so without our conscious knowledge, like the deep rudder of a boat. It's only once we bring them into the light that we can decide to do something differently.

When we've become aware, then we can experiment with making different choices. Maybe I decide to spend less time with that friend who's going through a crisis and who always leaves me feeling depleted. Maybe I pause for thirty seconds before I take the biscuits from the drawer. Maybe I keep eating the chocolate, but I stay curious about when I feel the urge to eat it and how my body feels afterwards. It can also be very powerful to make physical or structural changes – putting the biscuits in a drawer upstairs or not buying them in the first place, or scheduling half an hour recovery time after seeing our draining friend.

Here are some examples of things I do to change my conditions on purpose: regularly attend a 12 step group, choose to spend my time with friends who I can have a balanced relationship with, only check email once a day, go to Buddhist services, put time and energy into gardening, read spiritual books, have healthy snacks in the house, get rid of clothes that don't suit me or that don't fit properly, have a Buddha rupa next to my desk, keep our living room tidy. I don't manage all of these things all of the time, but when I do my life runs more smoothly and I tend to feel better about myself, which also helps me to be more present for other people.

Sometimes it is necessary to spend time in conditions that aren't conducive to our health. Our work might involve spending time with people who are suffering, or going into environments that are physically unpleasant. When this is the case, it is helpful to acknowledge the impact of these conditions on us. How did I feel after seeing that last patient? How is my back today? It also helps to build in regular spaces where we can come into contact with different conditions – weekly lunch with a sympathetic friend, or some quiet time when we get in from work to help us let go of our day. Remember radical responsibility – we are influenced by our conditions, but we always have a choice about how we respond to them. In Viktor Frankl's book 'Man's Search for Meaning' he shows how even in the very worst conditions of a concentration camp, it was possible for him to make choices that gave him a reason to go on and that allowed him to survive.

Tuning into our conditions and making choices to change them can have a radical effect on our life. When my husband Kaspa decided to move into The Buddhist House ten years ago, and when a few years later I signed up for their Buddhist psychotherapy course, who'd have thought that we'd end up together, happily running this beautiful temple in Malvern? Anything is possible. Change your conditions and let the magic start to work on you.

Questions for reflection

What conditions currently present in your life are healthy for you?

What conditions currently present in your life are unhealthy for you?

What do you do currently that you'd like to do more of?

What would you like to do less of?

Which people would you like to spend more time with? Less time with?

When is it particularly difficult for you to make a different choice? Can you bring kindness to this situation?

When are you likely to judge others for making 'bad decisions'? Can you imagine why it might be so difficult for them to make different decisions?

Where do you most resist the idea of radical responsibility?

What conditions tend to bring you joy?

What conditions would you like to change? How can you start making it happen?

Progress not perfection

All of you are perfect just as you are... and you could use a little improvement. ~ Suzuki Roshi

I would dearly love to be perfect. I've worked at it pretty hard for decades. I'm definitely making progress. I complete projects, I bake cakes for the sangha, I do my taxes on time, I eat a vegan diet, and I give money to charity. Of course, if you've read anything else in this book, you may also remember a few of the teensy weensy faults I'm still working on. I'm sure they'll be ironed out before too long, at which point I will become a Buddha and live happily ever after.

Most of us are afflicted by some form of perfectionism. Sometimes the expectations we have of ourselves are quite insidious. We might compare ourselves unfavourably to others, or feel envious of them. We might speak harshly to ourselves when we 'get things wrong' without being very conscious of it. We might project our unrealistic expectations of ourselves onto others, frequently feeling disappointed by the shortcomings of our friends, colleagues and groups.

'Progress not perfection' is a slogan taken from the 12 step programmes, and I am very grateful for it. It often comes to my mind. It corrects a tendency which many of us have – to feel discouraged whenever we decide to change ourselves and it takes longer than we want it to take. This discouragement can range from mild disappointment and frustration to full-blown hopelessness, rage and despair.

Whenever I notice myself falling into this trap, I remember these three words: progress not perfection. If we are making a small amount of progress, then we are making progress. Good! On some days I need to look further back into my past to see the progress. Yes, I'm still not looking after my body as well as I could be, but I have been doing yoga this year and I definitely feel more comfortable with my body than I did three years ago. Yes, I still struggle with self-care, but if I compare myself to the twenty year old me, I understand much more about my patterns and my needs.

What if we're not making progress, or even going backwards? When this happens, I like to practice withholding judgement. I don't know if these ten steps backwards are the precursor to thirty steps forwards or not. I do know that sometimes it has been necessary for me to dip more deeply into suffering in order to find a way forwards. That pain and lack of progress hasn't been what I have wanted, but when I look back with the benefit of hindsight it's been exactly what I've needed.

I've recently been through a difficult time with a work colleague. There have been issues in our relationship that have caused me a lot of pain – sleepless nights, deep confusion, and feelings of inadequacy and grief. I feel that I am beginning to emerge, and yesterday we had a long and honest conversation about what had been happening. I have learnt things about myself (my insecurities, how I keep myself safe) that I wouldn't have seen if it hadn't been for the particular buttons that were being pressed. The pain, in retrospect, seemed like a necessary signpost – encouraging me to look into dark places inside me where I didn't want to look. Now that I've brought some light to those places I'm a slightly different person – softer, humbler, more open-hearted, and braver.

We can never really know for sure what 'progress' even is. We might be eating more healthily but being grumpier with our husband as a result – is that progress? Experiencing a 'rock bottom' of some kind (with its accompanying trail of destruction) can be seen much later as the best thing that ever happened to us. Life is complex. Who knows what journey we're on, and what discomfort is necessary to get us to the most beautiful views? If we can, we can keep an open mind and trust that life is unfolding in its own way.

Why is perfection so seductive? Most of us have mixed motivations around wanting to be perfect. Some of these will be altruistic, as we hope to reduce the harm we cause other people. Others will be selfish, as we strive to protect ourselves or get more money or a good career or success or praise. For me, it is mostly about wanting to be in control. If I can stop making mistakes in public, then I don't have to expose myself to being judged ever again. If I can perfect my body, I won't have to get ill. If I can heal all my psychological issues, I'll always have harmony in my friendships and my marriage and I'll never have to be alone. We all want to avoid the messiness of being human.

Regardless of whether it's possible (and I'd suggest it's not!), I suspect that perfection is overrated. We tend to grow closer to people when we're brave enough to reveal our vulnerabilities to them, or they trust us with theirs. I've often found that surviving a difficulty in a relationship strengthens it like nothing else. Like the piece of grit in the oyster, beautiful pearls can form around our imperfections, as we find a way of transforming our particular fallibility into a gift.

If all else fails, we can always experiment with the idea that we are acceptable and loveable just as we are, regardless of whether we have improved or not. With our drinking-too-much, and with our mean streak. With our messy bedroom and our envy and our overspending and our bad morning breath. Yes, we could use a little improvement – no-one is denying that – but we are also all perfect just as we are.

Questions for reflection

When do you tend towards perfectionism? How does this make you feel?

When do you feel disappointed in yourself?

What tone of voice do you use with yourself when you feel you have failed?

When you next fall into thinking you should be perfect, can you check and see whether you've made any progress at all in this area of your life over the past month, year or ten years?

Do you ever project your hopes for perfection onto those around you and then feel disappointed by them?

How does it feel when you hear the phrase 'progress not perfection'? Do you resist it?

How is it to imagine that even if you don't make any progress you are acceptable just as you are?

Lean in

> *I let it go. It's like swimming against the current. It exhausts you. After a while, whoever you are, you just have to let go, and the river brings you home.*
> *~ Joanne Harris*

We lean on or into various objects, people and beliefs in our daily lives. I trust that the chair underneath me isn't going to disintegrate, and that my lungs are going to carry on their sweet work of keeping me alive. We depend on our friend to offer us a hug and a cup of coffee when we arrive at her house. We lean in to ideas about what will bring us happiness (possessions, success, leisure time, having children, praise) and how the world functions.

Sometimes leaning in works out well for us, and sometimes we fall flat on our faces. This is embarrassing, and it hurts. As time goes on we often solve this problem by deciding we don't need to lean on anything after all – we get excited at the idea of the self-perfection project, we are proud of our independence, and we trust less and less of the world. This keeps us safe (in a fashion), and it is understandable, but it exhausts us and it is doomed to fail.

Leaning in is delicious, frightening, and crucial. You can notice the physical difference between someone who holds themselves in, their shoulders tense and their gaze hypervigilant, and someone who owns their space, feeling secure in the moment. You can feel the difference yourself when you relax at the end of a yoga class and let your body slowly melt into the floor. If we don't allow ourselves to be supported, it is much more difficult to support others. If we don't lean in it is more difficult to learn about ourselves, to feel safe, to heal, to be nourished, and to feel joyfully connected to other people and to the world.

How can we begin to lean in more skilfully? Where do we go wrong? Earlier I wrote about a teaching central to Buddhism called The Three Marks of Being. The first two Marks of Being suggest that anything we encounter through the filter of our self-interest is impermanent and leads to dissatisfaction.

When we require things to be a certain way in order for us to be safe, we are setting ourselves up for trouble. If we need our husband to offer to do the washing up in order to feel loved, we will be upset when he doesn't offer. We try to manipulate people (especially our spouses!) to avoid being disappointed, and sometimes this brings results, but nobody wins when manipulation is involved. Whenever the other person isn't really bought in to whatever it is we want them to and they do it from a sense of duty or fear, they will generate some resentment which will emerge at some point. This happens with objects too – when we would prefer it if our new top fitted us and so we stretch it out of shape – and our beliefs – when we are invested in seeing ourselves as good cooks and so, when we burn the risotto, we don't mention it to our guests and everyone feels a bit awkward.

The third Mark of Being suggests that when we encounter things-as-they-are, rather than as we would like them to be, we have a true encounter with a reality which is non-self. This is what we can then lean into – something that is entirely not-us, something that is entirely Other. The word for things-as-they-are used in the original Sanskrit of the Three Marks is 'dharma', a word which generally refers to the teachings of the Buddha but also means something like 'the truth inherent in all things'. When we let go of our preoccupation with self, we can lean in to dharma – to something in the Universe which we can rely on, and which will support us.

This means leaning into our actual husband, rather than the version who offers to do the washing up, and maybe also being more honest with ourselves about our insecurities around whether he cares. It means taking our top back and changing it for a size up, and feeling the disappointment that we're not as slender as we used to be. It means apologising for the burnt risotto and being freed up to have a laugh about it with your guests.

As Buddhists we hold that the very best thing to lean into is the thing that is not impermanent. I'm thinking of a badge I saw on a sangha member's jacket: 'Believe in Good'. We might use different words to describe this 'Good' – the numinous, God, the Good in the Universe, or a Higher Power. It doesn't matter too much what it is or how we conceptualise it. What matters is that we are open to the possibility of there being something in the Universe that isn't us; something that it is Good, and that we can lean into it.

Until we reach a point where we only lean into Dharma, which won't happen until we're a Buddha, then we will continue to be disappointed. I wish it were otherwise. People will let us down, objects will shatter, and we will fall onto our faces. We will be hurt, and that's okay. We will survive. Lie under a tree and lean back into the earth's green chest. Extend the hand of friendship to a cranky colleague. Go to a concert and let the music hold you. Make yourself vulnerable in a safe group. Find places to lean in. Get up when you fall – shake yourself off, give your bruises a chance to heal – and then lean in again.

Questions for reflection

What thoughts and feelings moved through you as you read this chapter?

What do you currently lean into? Money? Family? Praise? Failure? What else?

How do you see people, places and things through the lens of your self-centred fear? How could you see them (and begin to accept them) more as-they-are?

What would you like to practice leaning into more?

When have you leaned in and then fallen a long way and been very hurt? What thoughts, feelings or beliefs has this left you with? How might you bring some healing to this hurt?

When did you last fall? What happened?

Do you know any people (in your life, in books etc.) who lean in?

How do they live? What do you like or admire about their lives?

Do you have some sense of leaning into what's not impermanent? How could you begin to explore this, or strengthen your connection with your Higher Power?

What could you lean into right now?

Attend to others

> *Those who are unhappy have no need for anything in this world but people capable of giving them their attention. The capacity to give one's attention to a sufferer is a very rare and difficult thing; it is almost a miracle; it is a miracle. Nearly all those who think they have this capacity do not possess it. Warmth of heart, impulsiveness, pity are not enough.* ~ Simone Weil

As Weil says, we are generally not highly skilled at attending to others. Whilst the other person is talking, we are formulating what we would like to say next. We interrupt. We discount what they are saying before they've finished, or we tune out. We listen to them through our many self-centred filters, making assumptions about what they mean or deciding what would be good for them. This is especially likely if the other person is going through something similar to something we've been through – we think we 'know what it's like' without listening out for the differences in their experience as well as the similarities.

We also tend to shrink away from their pain, anger or sadness. It is very difficult to be present with another's suffering without wanting to hurry them out of it. We don't like to see someone in pain, especially when we care about them. We may also become consciously or unconsciously reminded of our own pain, which causes us to veer away. When we witness strong emotion in others we often find ourselves moving from listening mode into persuasion, avoidance or defence.

What I want when I am in pain isn't for someone to say 'it's not really so bad, cheer up' or 'that reminds me of the time I...' or 'don't you think you should...'. What I want is: 'ouch, I can hear how horrible that is'. I don't need the other person to start telling me how I can fix it, and I don't want them to feel panicked by my distress. I want them to sit quietly with me and accompany me as we walk through my story at my own pace.

As a psychotherapist I have had lots of practice at offering this to others, and I still find it difficult. I am generally comfortable sitting with people who are in deep pain, but it's much more uncomfortable for me to sit with people's anger. Sometimes I catch myself ushering them away from it – changing the subject, or suggesting that they soften their view about someone who has upset them – to save myself from being in the presence of their fury. We all have our ways of ushering people this way and that way, subtly or not so subtly giving signals to people about what we'd prefer they talk about or feel and what we'd definitely prefer they didn't.

When we listen properly, we are opening up a sacred space for a person where they can share their experience with no fear of being judged or manipulated. If their sadness takes them under, we go under with them. If they get frustrated with us or with the world, we allow them to fully express it and we hear it. We don't talk them out of their experience, whether it tallies with our own or not. We stay curious, we check out whether we've heard them properly (most simply by repeating what they say back to them in our own words), and we leave lots of silent spaces. We put our own agenda on hold.

Oh, how difficult this can be. But oh, what a wonderful offering it makes. What a privilege it is when the other begins to trust us, and to share a little bit more of their tender spots. Proper listening, a complete gifting of our attention to others, is like a kind of magic. Under the conditions of being-listened-to, people unfurl like snowdrop petals into the cold winter air. If we wait patiently and allow them to unfold in their own time, we will witness their beauty.

Questions for reflection

How often do you really attend to others?

What are your worst listening habits?

Can you remember a time when you did really listen? How did the other person receive this listening?

When do you find it most difficult to listen? When the other person is being angry, boring, needy, sad, bossy? When this next happens, give yourself empathy as your buttons get pressed. If you can, wonder about what might be underneath the other person's anger, boring-ness etc.

When do you find yourself becoming more judgemental when you're listening? How can you notice these judgements and put them aside in order to really understand how it is for the other person?

Can you listen out for what someone might be trying to communicate behind their words?

When you don't have the capacity to listen, how could you kindly let the other person know that it isn't a good time for you?

Who in your life needs you to stop trying to change them and start listening to them?

How well do you listen to yourself? How could you spend more time listening to yourself?

Who do you need to attend to today?

Seek sangha

> *Everyone I meet is in my sangha. I don't know if that's the proper definition, but that's the way I'm going to hold it in my mind.* ~ Jeff Bridges

In Buddhism we take refuge in the three jewels – the Buddha, the Buddha's teachings, and the community of people who follow the Buddha's teachings. This last jewel is called sangha. The Buddha advised us to find a sangha because it is very difficult to stay on our spiritual path, especially when it twists and turns and goes through patches of thorns, without the support of people who are also on the path.

I have formed a mini-sangha this week with three writers who are in the same building as me, working on their own manuscripts – two novels and a children's story. We met on Thursday night, and now it is Saturday. We sit in our little apartments all day, staring at our screens and searching for the right words. In the evenings we eat together and share our experience of the day. It is supremely helpful to know that there are other people engaged in a similar task to me, and that they are getting on with it. They booked themselves on to this retreat because, like me, they think their writing is important. We are honouring that by staying put at our desks even when we would rather go to the cinema or, frankly, anywhere other than continuing to untangle these knots of words.

Our sangha doesn't have to be a spiritual group. Any group with good ethics at its heart and which supports us in our life-tasks will do. An old psychotherapy client of mine joined a Tae Kwondo group, and being a part of this group offered her more than anything I could have done. She began to smile at people and be recognised, and slowly moved from extreme isolation to being stitched into warm community for the first time in her life. My friend Iszi volunteers for the Wildlife Trust and spends a good portion of her weekends planting hedges or clearing land with her colleagues. My friend Sujatin has a knitting-sangha.

The best sanghas contain at least a few people we'd like to emulate. If you admire their sense of humour or their wisdom, then hanging around with them will give you a good chance of some of it rubbing off on you.

We lean into our sanghas gradually. It makes us vulnerable to lean into groups and begin to trust them. Sometimes you begin with a honeymoon period, but as time goes on we're likely to feel a bit or a lot let down by individuals in the group or by the whole group. If we stick around any group for long enough, just like sticking around any person, their flaws become more apparent. What we took for solidity turns out to be stuckness, and the humour we coveted now seems like it might be a defence against intimacy. We also begin to identify the differences between ourselves and others in the group, or between our values and norms and the culture of the group.

It's always important to give ourselves the option of leaving if we feel we're not in a healthy environment. It can also be a good thing to have some sticking power when things get difficult. My own spiritual sangha went through a very difficult phase when my Buddhist teacher split up with his wife of twenty years – people were pulled in various directions and at one point it felt like the whole thing might fragment. Most of us came out on the other side, and our relationships have been strengthened as a result of this time of difficulty – much as a hardened-off seedling has a better chance of survival.

My various sanghas (Buddhist, 12 Step, writers) inspire me, challenge me and look after me. Sometimes they drive me crazy – as I'm sure I drive them crazy. They are rich places to learn about others and to learn about myself. They improve over time as we learn to resolve conflicts and as we become more deeply fond of each other, with all of our faults. I am always grateful to them. Homage to the Sangha!

Questions for reflection

How is it to be a member of your biological family? What feels good? What doesn't feel good? What have you learnt about being in groups from your family?

What have you received from sanghas in the past?

What sanghas do you currently belong to?

What do you appreciate about them?

Are there any sanghas that you need to get into a healthier relationship with, take time away from or even leave?

In what areas of your life would you like to feel more supported? Your creative life? Your spiritual life?

Where could you seek out new sanghas that would support you? If there isn't one that fits the bill, could you create it?

Do you have any patterns that tend to repeat themselves when you are in groups? How could you bring some more light to these patterns?

Do you tend towards isolating yourself or leaning too heavily on others when you are having difficulties? How could you take a step towards the middle way?

Which group, past or present, would you like to feel grateful for right now?

Make offerings

> *I like cats a lot. I've always liked cats. They're great company. When they eat, they always leave a little bit at the bottom of the bowl. A dog will polish the bowl, but a cat always leaves a little bit. It's like an offering. ~ Christopher Walken*

Recently a member of our Buddhist group told me she was sitting in front of her little shrine when she remembered that she could make an offering to the Buddha. She hadn't done this before. Making offerings is a ritual that Buddhists all around the world perform – pouring water into bowls for the Buddha to 'drink', lighting an incense stick for the sweet smoky scent, or offering the light of candle flame. As she performed her ritual, she had a strong and unexpected sense of the Buddha receiving her intentions, and her heart opened up.

Children instinctively make offerings to those they love, stashing a shell or an autumn leaf in their pocket to take home to their grandfather, or bringing pictures proudly home from school. Sometimes as adults we lose this natural impulse to offer gifts. We begin to think of gift-giving as one side of a transaction or equation which must be equally balanced. This is especially the case at Christmas, as we try to work out how much money to spend on each person, and how much our presents look like they're worth. Have I given this person enough? Will they like it? Will I receive enough in return?

This kind of calculation is an attempt at protecting ourselves from both the receiver's and our own disappointment or judgement. Both as giver and receiver, we can confuse the gift's financial worth or appropriateness with how much the other person cares about us, and what value they put on us. Giving presents leaves us at risk of 'getting it wrong'. Our gift might be accompanied by resentment too, as we hand something over to a relative we're in a complicated relationship with, or we spend money that we don't really have.

I recently received the gift of a picture from a sangha member which wasn't to my taste at all. After feeling initially awkward (what would I do with it? Would they expect to see it on my walls?) I relaxed into feeling delighted. It wasn't an object that I was going to keep, but I completely received the sentiment behind the giving – the care they'd taken in choosing it, and the warm feelings towards me that the gift represented. The actual object is irrelevant – it's great when we do receive something that we find beautiful or useful, but if we don't we can pass it on to someone who does (making them happy too) and fully receive the spirit of the offering instead.

When I was away from home recently I found a tiny bright red button that had fallen from my clothes. It was such a perfect thing. I spontaneously gave it to the little Buddha I'd brought along with me, resting it in his hands. The Buddha is a good person to make offerings to as he's always pleased – just look at his smile! We can practice make offerings to anyone and anything – people, special places, various deities or the spirit of nature. We can enjoy being creative and trust that we will be received. Offerings can be objects, cups of tea, stroking our rabbits or smiling at strangers. We could see tidying the garden or composting our vegetable peelings as an offering to nature, and our work as an offering to all the customers our company serves.

At the beating heart of every offering is the spirit in which it is made. We never make offerings because we want to curry the favour of the Gods, or anyone else. We do it because we feel moved to, like a young boy wanting to make his mother happy. Our offering is freely made – we expect nothing in return, not even the gratitude of the receiver. The offering is powered by gratitude – our own. Enjoy making offerings, both formally and spontaneously. If you're lucky you might feel your own heart opening, as our sangha member did, connecting her to the ocean of light and love.

Questions for reflection

What or who would you like to make a small offering to? It doesn't matter if it's a real person, a book, your pets, nature or the Universe.

What could you offer?

Are there any rituals that you would like to perform alongside your offering?

Would you like to start the habit of making regular offerings? You could bow towards the sun to say thank you before you start working in your veggie patch, or light incense every morning for all the Good in the Universe.

Could you make a small offering to someone or something right now?

Take refuge

> *Why does one go for refuge? Because the body is unreliable, the emotions are unreliable, the mind is unreliable and the world is on fire with greed, hate and delusion. This is the core of Buddha's teaching.*
> ~ Dharmavidya David Brazier

Our flat is the bottom floor of our four storey temple, the bottom two of which are below street level, cut into the Malvern hills. One of our cats Roshi has always been afraid of venturing up to the ground floor, where the cars roar past the windows like monsters and frighten him back downstairs. Last night I was waiting for people to arrive to our usual Wednesday night Buddhist service and I heard Roshi meowing from downstairs. He was lonely, and he could hear me upstairs, on the floor he's too scared to visit. I went halfway down the stairs and crouched on the landing, talking to him in a low voice. He ran up the hazardous stairs and disappeared inside my robe, where he promptly lay down and purred loudly.

Taking refuge is like finding a robe that we can disappear into – a place where we feel safe. The world is frightening. Instead of car-monsters we are faced with heart attacks, floods, muggers, heartbreak, financial catastrophes... As an attempt at protecting ourselves from all this, or at least try to forget about it all for a while, we all take refuge in all sorts of things. We watch television and eat crisps, we take out insurance policies and sit on piles of money, we make friends with powerful people and build our career.

These forms of refuge all bring us relief to a lesser or greater degree. As Dharmavidya says above, they are all ultimately unreliable – but that doesn't mean that we can't continue to lean into them. Some things are healthier to take refuge in than others – video games vs. extra-marital affairs or body-building vs. heroin. One thing we can do is begin to identify some of our unhealthier refuges, judged by the negative impact they have on different areas of our life such as our health or our relationships, and slowly swap them for different ones. If you can't afford your owning-a-horse refuge any more, maybe see if you can do some volunteer work at a stable.

Special places can work particularly well as refuges. One of my friends takes refuge in the sea, and whenever her life is difficult she either brings the sea to mind or takes a trip to the seaside. Another friend has a special connection with the standing stones at Avebury. If we visit these places every so often, we can keep them with us even when we're far away – conjuring up the landscape and remembering how we felt when we were there. We can also use people, whether we know them or not, and whether they are alive or dead, as refuges. We can connect with what that person might say to us, how they had faith in us, or how we used to feel when we were around them.

Buddhism says that the ultimate refuge can be found outside the impermanent material world, with your Higher Power or with some sense of everything-being-okay. If this isn't something you currently connect with, experiment by developing a small ritual which you can return to when you're feeling groundless or afraid. This might simply be taking three slow breaths and imagining the earth under your feet supporting you, or turning towards the sun, or saying the name of your Higher Power or a short inspirational verse, or sitting in meditation for a short while. You may not feel anything at first (except self-conscious) – persevere for a few weeks and see what happens.

Once after meditation I had a very strong image of a warm orange light surrounding me. It was all around me and it moved as I moved, but there was a very small gap between it and my skin – I wasn't touching it. I knew that all I had to do to touch it was to relax and lean slightly – in any direction – and I would be held. Just like Roshi, relaxing inside the warm cave of my robe. This is how refuge feels for me. Whether or not I feel the comfort of that orange light against my skin I know that it's there, and I know that it holds me safe.

Questions for reflection

How is it to imagine yourself as a refugee, without any permanent home here in this impermanent world?

What do you currently take refuge in? Make a list.

How do these various refuges work for you?

Are there any refuges that are currently causing you or others harm?

If you want to step away from these refuges, what could you begin to replace them with?

Where are your safe spaces?

Do you have any sense of any refuges which are not impermanent? What does this look or feel like for you?

Could you develop a little ritual to connect you with your Higher Power?

Honour work

> *When contemplating what our life's work might be, we are often driven by our attachment to security. Perhaps the one question we don't ask often enough is "What do I have to offer?"*
> ~Ezra Bayda

I just received a big package in the post. Inside were 27 pieces of paper, some handwritten, some typed, each one a thank you letter from an eleven year old who visited the temple last month. 'My favourite instrument was the singing bowl, I loved feeling the vibrations on my hands.' 'I was stunned that it took three people to carry the statue of the Buddha.' 'The meditation was really hard because Rosie started laughing.' 'You were really nice to us. Love from your friend Alfredo.'

Reading these letters is pure nectar. When I first started doing talks to schools, I dreaded it. I didn't have much experience of working with children, and I didn't know how to keep their attention or how to deal with it when they got fidgety and giggly. I got nervous beforehand and was sweaty and exhausted by the end. I could have handed all these school visits over to a colleague, but I trusted that I had something to learn, and so I kept doing them. How could I best offer service as a Priest in front of a class? I gradually overcame my fear, and I began to find out what worked and what didn't. These sessions still leave me knackered, but I find them a real privilege these days, and receiving these letters has touched my heart.

I was lucky enough to grow up in a family and a culture that gave me some choices about what I wanted to do for a living. I started work more than twenty years ago in the Call Centre of a financial services company, telling people how much they had in their savings account and dealing with complaints. Over time I discovered the things I loved doing and headed towards jobs where I'd get to do more of them. I enjoyed helping people to learn and grow, and so worked towards being a Customer Services Coach in the same company, and then went on to train as a therapist. I was in love with words, and so wrote poems and then my first novel by getting up an hour early and writing before I went to work.

My life today consists of a wide variety of different work which I find deeply gratifying. Some of this work pays and some of it doesn't pay at all, and that feels fine. I feel I've arrived here through a combination of good karma and of many years of little intentional actions. I chose the stars I wanted to follow – writer, psychotherapist – and set about doing the right training, studying, living for periods without much money, applying for new jobs, and stepping out of my comfort zone. It took courage, perseverance and faith but, because I was following my stars, I enjoyed the journey very much.

I've slowly worked towards the work that I *want* to do, but I also believe that being a writer, a psychotherapist and a Priest is also the best work I have to offer the world. We are more likely to do a good job if we feel inspired and nourished by what we're doing. I had the potential to train as a doctor, and if I was a doctor I would definitely save more lives, but I wouldn't enjoy doing it, and so I'd be mediocre at best. We can use our 'ought' will-power or a desire for money or status as our motivation in the short term, but it's difficult to sustain an entire career on these flimsy foundations. A good career, like everything else, has to be built on love.

If we are in full time employment until retirement age, we will end up working around 90 thousand hours. This is 35% of our waking hours during our working years. This is a very large chunk of time! Are you stuck in a job you're not enjoying, or do you feel trapped by your financial responsibilities? Do you feel what you'd really like to do is out of reach?

My first suggestion is that you stay where you are, unless you are being harmed by something or someone. In my experience, it's sensible to learn what we need to learn before we move on, like levels in a video game. I know that my years in the Call Centre taught me good customer service, as well as how to deal with tedium and how to keep myself self-motivated. What might your lessons be before you move on? What skills or qualities do you need to develop? Like me in front of a class of children, begin to wonder about how you could best be of service in this role. It doesn't matter if it feels meaningful to you or not – how can you make your colleague's lives easier? How can you make your customers happy? Could you make your work environment more beautiful? If you are unhappy about the culture of your workplace, how could you start demonstrating an alternative?

Once you've seen what you need to learn in your current situation, you can start thinking about which star you'd like to follow. Are you called to work with animals? Would you like to do what you're doing now but for a more ethical company?

Would you like the freedom (and responsibility) of being self-employed? The Buddha spoke about 'Right Livelihood' as a way of bringing our ethical ideals to work. In the Vanijja Sutta it says: "A lay follower should not engage in five types of business. Which five? Business in weapons, business in human beings, business in meat, business in intoxicants, and business in poison." What parts of your current livelihood do you feel uncomfortable about? What is your version of Right Livelihood? What do you dream of doing?

Whatever you are doing now, whether you are working for money or not, it is always possible to make a positive difference to those around us. We need to be realistic about our capacity, remembering that we have unique strengths and weaknesses like every other human being. Sometimes we'll improve, and sometime we won't manage to. That's okay. Sometimes we get affirmation, like my package of letters, and often we don't. That's okay – planting good seeds always leads to blossoms, even if we rarely see them. By caring for ourselves, for others and for the planet we can honour our work and do the best job we can do.

Questions for reflection

How do you feel about your current work?

How meaningful is it?

Do you feel that it is a 'Right Livelihood' for you?

How could you make more of the work you're in right now?

What do you have to learn from the work you're in right now?

What bits of your job do you enjoy?

What holds you back at work? Which of these things do you have some control over? How could you start working on these things?

What have you always dreamed of doing?

Would you like to choose a star to orient yourself by, with the long-term aim of spending more of your time doing particular things either in your work or leisure time?

What good seeds have you planted in the past? Can you imagine that they might lead to good even if you don't see it?

How can you care better for yourself, others and the world? How could you bring this attitude into your work?

Make mistakes

> *In fact, life is mostly one mistake after another. The attempt to be always in the right or to get a perfect formula is self-defeating. There is too much going on. The attempt to always be in the perfectly balanced attitude is paralysing. When we walk along it works because we are always off balance. If we were not we would not move forward. The art of Buddhism is not to stand stock still, but rather to use the imbalance of life to flow onward. Thus the Buddhas take us just as we are, not in a state of frozen fear of getting things wrong.*
> *~ Dharmavidya David Brazier*

Yesterday I made a mistake. I individually copy-pasted a message to hundreds of people in a group I help manage, letting them know about an important weekly meeting. This morning I checked a reply from someone and my stomach sank. I'd written the wrong time for the meeting! I've been attending this meeting for a long time – how could I have got the most important detail wrong? I had wasted at least two hours of my time and, worse, shown myself up in front of all those people.

I knew it wasn't the end of the world, but for a while I felt just terrible. The shame pulsed through me and I felt frustrated and upset with myself. I really don't want to be the kind of person who makes basic errors in public. I desperately searched for a way to shift the responsibility onto something or someone else – is it because I was tired? Could I blame my cat, for distracting me as I wrote the message? It felt like there was a battle going on inside me, as I tried to maintain my identity as 'a professional who always pays attention to detail', and as the reality of the mistake kept bashing holes in it.

It wasn't a comfortable process. What helped was to remind myself that it is in the nature of human beings to get things wrong. We all make mistakes – almost continuous teensy weensy ones, a rash of middle sized ones, and the occasional whopping ones that ruin lives. Poor creatures – we can't help it! We can take sensible precautions to guard against them – not driving when we're very tired, or triple checking messages that go out to hundreds of people – but we'll never be able to eliminate them entirely.

What also helps is to own our mistakes as fully as we can, to feel contrition, and to make amends if we can. Once I had stopped blaming the cat, I was able to say to myself: 'You have made a silly error, sweetheart, as you are prone to do. I can hear that you feel terrible about it. You didn't mean to do it, and it's not the end of the world. Now how can you put it right?' I started to message the people I'd heard from, apologising and being clear about the correct time. I put a note on the main group page. I immediately started to feel better.

What if we're in a situation where we do regret our behaviour, but we also think that the other party or parties should regret their own behaviour at least as much? When we're not the only person at fault, it can feel like we're letting the other person off the hook if we apologise for what we did.

I'd encourage you to apologise anyway, being clear about what you did that you regret. We can take responsibility for, e.g. raising our voice at someone, even if we were provoked. You're not just apologising for the other person's sake, you're apologising as a way of 'keeping your own side of the street clean'. It's good to be able to walk down our side of the street without tripping over our junk – even the air smells cleaner. Whether or not the other takes responsibility for their own unskilful behaviour in this particular situation, you can trust that their karma will continue to unfold and they'll be faced with the consequences of their actions at some point. Hand them back to their Higher Power and, as Jesus suggested, attend to the log in your own eye before worrying about the splinter in theirs.

When I first started learning to drive at the age of seventeen, my arms and legs wouldn't do what I wanted them to do. I felt bad, and apologised to my driving instructor over and over again. My instructor told me that I shouldn't say sorry, I should say 'oops'. All these years later, I feel moved by his kindness. He knew how it was to be a vulnerable learner, and he wanted to give me permission to make as many mistakes as I needed to make – that's how I would learn to drive. 'Sorry' is 'I messed it up again, I'm failing you.' 'Oops' is 'there I go again, stalling at a roundabout... okay, let's try again'. See if you can catch your beating-yourself-up sorrys, and try instead for oops.

Most of us do survive our mistakes, and go on to make them again. Sometimes we even learn something, and then make different ones. In this way we lurch forwards, knocking things over, the heat rushing to our cheeks and then fading away. Sometimes we can make direct amends, and sometimes things stay broken. Sometimes our mistakes even become the best thing that ever happened to us. They're not going anywhere, so we may as well make friends with them. Give them a cup of cocoa and a big fat hug.

Questions for reflection

What was the last mistake you made? How did it make you feel?

How often do you own your mistakes and make amends?

What stories do you tell yourself or other people about your mistakes?

What feels like the worst thing about making mistakes?

How is it when you observe other people making mistakes? Is there anyone you admire who always owns their mistakes?

How would it be to acknowledge that mistakes are a part of how we move forwards?

Have you made any mistakes in the past which you'd like to face up to? Do you have any overdue amends to make? How do you think it would affect your life if you began to do this? What has stopped you so far – what are you afraid of?

How can you practice being kinder to yourself when you next mess up? Don't worry, you probably won't have to wait too long to try it out!

Lighten up

As soon as you have made a thought, laugh at it.
~ Lao Tsu

I heard a story about the Dalai Lama a long time ago which I like to think is true. He was standing ceremoniously on stage in front of a huge eager crowd, ready to dispense his wisdom. He began by pronouncing some fact or other. Before he could carry on his assistant, who was standing next to him, tugged on his robes to get his attention and suggested humbly that he was mistaken. I imagine the microphone picking up the assistant's words and sending them out into the crowd. The Dalai Lama brushed him off, feeling certain of what he was saying, and continued. Once again his assistant interrupted, respectfully, and said that he'd got it wrong. Again the Dalai Lama dismissed him, maybe sharing an indulgent smile with the crowd.

It was only when the assistant had stopped him a third time that the penny dropped. He *was* wrong! There was an awkward silence, and I imagine the crowd holding their breath – what would he do? Surely he must be embarrassed? Would he scold the assistant, or pretend that nothing had happened? What he did was to throw back his head and laugh. He laughed at himself – at how his pride had prevented him from hearing his assistant, and at how he'd been exposed in front of all these people. The laughter cleansed him of embarrassment and brought him back to the teaching he was there to do.

One of my favourite things about my Buddhist teacher Dharmavidya is that he chuckles all the time. When we are together as a group, it is infectious. This laughter is most often directed towards himself, as he is deeply amused at the ridiculousness of the human condition. Being sure of the deep fondness he has for us, our laughter is sparked as we see that we are foolish too.

This kind of wry laughter softens the often painful experience of being fallible and vulnerable. It brings us together and it makes our failings seem less terrible, more inevitable, and more forgivable. It also feels good to laugh so hard that your belly aches.

This is the kind of laughter that brings our egos down to their proper size, rather than laughter that props us up. This propping-up humour makes us feel better about ourselves because we feel taller when we are treading on someone else. Some comedians specialise in this kind of humour – the joke is always on someone else. Laughter that props us up will always have a trace of guilt mixed in. We guess how it would feel to be the person on the receiving end, and so it doesn't feel good to be on the other side. Humour can also be misused in other ways – to avoid intimacy, or to demand attention.

Lightening up doesn't mean that we neglect emotions from different parts of the palette, or that we experience life any less intensely. My first residential poetry course was tutored by the late poet Adrian Mitchell. I fell in love with him a little – he was kind to us, and he felt things deeply. Once when we were out walking across the moors he quietly picked up a piece of rubbish and put it into his pocket to take back to the house, just because it was there. On the third night he read his poems to us. He started with the poem about his small daughter holding out her hand to him to walk her up the stairs, and how he wished the stairs would go on forever. As I write I'm remembering hearing the emotion in his voice and it brings tears of tenderness, just as it did when I was there. At the end of his next poem he had us roaring with laughter. A few poems later there were more tears, this time tears of bitter grief, and then soon we were laughing again. He was able to bring so much to life in us because he was full of life himself, and emotion flowed through him like dry sand through a tube.

We can always bring a lightness of touch to whatever is happening. I have been to funerals where a knowing joke about the deceased has brought the mourners together in their fond memories. We can catch ourselves when we begin to get too serious, solemn or self-important, and smile a wry, fond smile at ourselves. Or maybe we'll make a bigger mistake, and we can really throw back our heads and laugh.

Questions for reflection

When did you last laugh?

How often do you laugh with friends, family or colleagues?

How often do you smile at yourself?

Do you associate humour with putting other people down?

When do you tend to be over-serious or heavy?

Is there a current difficult situation which you could bring some lightness to? What might the lightness illuminate?

What makes you smile? How could you bring more of this to your life?

Radical honesty

> *I want to unfold.*
> *I don't want to stay folded anywhere,*
> *because where I am folded, there I am a lie.*
> *~ Rainer Maria Rilke*

I am on a writing retreat in Shropshire, and a tea-light is currently burning in my candle-holder. The heart shaped holder was a present from my good poet friend Esther more than a decade ago, and it lights the way for me whenever I write. I haven't asked the retreat centre manager whether or not I can burn candles in my room. I could have mentioned it during our welcome talk but I was afraid of being told 'no', and so I noticed the opportunity in a moment of silence and let it pass.

I have been carrying this little half-lie with me, and in that place I am folded. The light can't get in, and there is a crease developing. This is the first disadvantage of lying – it doesn't feel good. We might feel a flush of pleasure when we 'get away with something', but it is the kind of thrill we feel when our enemy fails, or when we eat more apple crumble than we should. The layer of excitement is covering up something like sadness or anger or upset, and the pleasure inevitably leads to a hangover of some kind.

This omission is also damaging the relationship I have with the centre manager. I know that I ought to ask her, and this creates a little barrier between us. On a subtle energetic level she will know that I am holding something back. We intuit more from each other than we realise, and then use this information unconsciously when deciding how much to trust each other or how far out of our way we'll go for each other. Withholding the truth or lying has an effect on whoever we come into contact with, the folded ripples going out into the world and casting a faint shadow on whatever they encounter.

I am using a minor example of lying here – maybe it's all I can admit to this morning! – but we are all engaged in much larger story-fabrication projects in various areas of our lives. We might be busy fooling our boss that we're feeling confident about something that we're actually terrified by, or pretending to our spouse that we're unaffected by their complaints about us. We fool ourselves a lot of the time too, when the truth might lead to inconvenience or imagined catastrophe – when we're in denial about our addictions, when we have affairs, when we convince ourselves that we can carry on juggling too many balls. If you notice that you repeat the same story about yourself to a few people, there is probably a folded part in there somewhere.

When we decide to (or are forced to) 'come clean', we generally do feel cleaner afterwards. We might feel profound relief, regret, resentment or vulnerability. It's sometimes the beginning of a period of contrition as we begin to make amends for the pain our lies or our actions have caused. Whatever the consequences, we have an opportunity to come into a more authentic relationship with others and with ourselves, and the energy we've been using to keep the lie folded away is freed up to flow into other things.

Should we always tell the truth? In the 12 Step programme we are taken through a process of identifying and admitting where we have caused harm to others, and then making amends to them. Step 9 says: "Made direct amends to such people wherever possible, except when to do so would injure them or others." This is a good rule of thumb for telling the truth. We need to think carefully about whether our truth will harm the other person unnecessarily, and also make sure that we are making amends for the other person's benefit rather than just wanting the relief of getting it off our chests. If in doubt, pause – discuss it with people you trust, and wait for clarity before you act.

After typing the first few paragraphs of this chapter, I blew my candle out. Bringing my attention to this little lie had shown me how uncomfortable it felt, and had taken the good writing magic out of the flame. Later I walked the five minutes over to the retreat centre office where I checked with the manager about whether it was okay to burn candles in my room. She said it was fine. It's burning now, just to the left of the keyboard, and it is burning more happily. The fold is unfolded, and light can get in.

Questions for reflection

How honest are you?

How honestly did you answer the previous question?!

Where are there currently folds or lies in your life?

What effect do these lies have on you? On others?

What lies do you tell about yourself to others?

What lies do you tell about yourself to yourself?

What would you like to confess? To whom?

Who do you lie to because you think it protects them from something?

Who would you like to made amends to?

What are you afraid might happen if you started to tell the truth more?

How does it feel when you tell the truth or confess to an untruth?

When other people tell the truth, how does it make you feel?

What is true about you right now?

When you can't stop it, clock it

> *...the actual or potential alcoholic, with hardly any exception, will be absolutely unable to stop drinking on the basis of self-knowledge. This is a point we wish to emphasize and re-emphasize, to smash home upon our alcoholic readers as it has been revealed to us out of bitter experience.*
> ~ *The Big Book of Alcoholics Anonymous*

Last night I spoke in our Listening Circle about the realisation that, when I had set my mind upon buying some expensive chocolates earlier in the week, it would have been very difficult to stop me. An urge had arisen to order some Duffy's, which I hadn't eaten for a long time. If you had tried to get between me and the computer in that moment, after you'd given up trying to reason with me, you might have had to use physical force...

    The feeling rang alarm bells in me. I don't think it's a bad thing in itself to order high quality chocolate – I can afford it at the moment, and the money will go to support the chocolatier as well as the farmers they buy their fair-trade cocoa beans from. I enjoy the chocolate very much. However, the intense feeling of not-wanting-to-stop was a warning. It signalled that the part of me buying the chocolate was afraid of being stopped – not by others, as I hid in my room to make the online purchase! – but by other parts of me.

If I'd stopped to listen, what would these other parts of me have had to say? They would have gently pointed out that I'd put in two orders for chocolate online already that week, and the orders hadn't yet arrived. They would have reminded me that I had spent quite a lot of money over the past week on chocolate and books – and that maybe I could take a little break from spending. If I'd sat down and had a cup of tea with myself, I might have uncovered some of the drive behind the compulsive behaviour – some anxiety about an upcoming retreat, a week of being 'internet sober' again and only checking email and Facebook once a day, and maybe some sadness about a recent visit to a sick friend.

Our behaviour can develop an urgent, almost violent quality when we are entranced by a compulsion which 'keeps us safe' from something. We may be able to make a link between our behaviour and something difficult that's happening in our lives, and we may not. Sometimes compulsions take on a life of their own and, like a rat pressing on a bar to receive heroin, we just keep on buying the chocolate, regardless of whether it still brings us pleasure or relief. We know that compulsions and addictions progress to a point where there's hardly any relief mixed in with the grief and damage at all – food addiction leads to obesity, sex addiction leads to broken laws or marriages, substance addiction leads to the loss of dignity, children, hope, and sometimes lives.

I'm lucky in that my 'favourite' addictions (food, workaholism, the internet) are relatively benign. They haven't yet progressed to a stage where they've threatened relationships, my health or my livelihood. Even so, it makes a staggering difference to my daily life when I manage to engage with the internet in a healthy way. Rather than waking up and diving into my phone, seeing who has emailed me in the night, I wake up and enter the day more gently. My mind is less fragmented, and my days feel extravagantly spacious, even if I have a lot to do. I can read a book without flicking my eyes to my phone every few minutes. I can live!

We all use various substances, behaviours and activities to help us avoid uncomfortable feelings. We might use them in different ways on different days. Most of the time I have a healthy relationship with food and I enjoy eating – it nourishes me physically, emotionally and spiritually. Sometimes I binge on sugar and wake up in the morning feeling sluggish and sick. I also have a mixed relationship with spending money, working and getting things done, the television, and getting people to like me. Sometimes a funny film or an easy-to-read detective novel is just what I need to relax at the end of a busy weekend. Sometimes I hide in a book when I know it would be more helpful to put the book down and go and do the thing I don't want to do.

This last example points us towards the disadvantage of all our compulsive behaviour, regardless of whether it's still working as an anaesthetic or not. 'Acting out' is a step to the side. We are avoiding something, and this something will not go away if we get drunk or have an affair. If I am avoiding a difficult conversation with my husband by reading, the shortest way to relief is actually to put the book down and have the conversation (or at least start working on the problem more directly, for example by getting some advice from a friend). It's the scariest way, but it's the only way to tackle it once and for all.

If you're wondering about how healthy your behaviour is at any time, check in with yourself by asking 'how easily could I stop right now?' If the answer involves someone literally dragging you away by your leg, like me and the chocolate-buying, then you can get curious. What has been happening in the past few days or in the past hour? If you sit down quietly for a few moments before you succumb to the urge, what do you notice in your body? Tension? Any feelings? If you were to ask yourself what you need, and allow all the different bits of you to speak (not just the bit that wants the ice-cream) what would they all say?

This practice is about noticing what we are up to. In my experience, change happens of its own accord when we bring gentle awareness to the full complexities of the problem. You could also practise stopping when you notice your reluctance to stop. Start small, with something you don't have a great compulsion to do. Maybe you're with a friend when a juicy piece of gossip comes to mind. The urge is to mention it… Notice, and refrain from sharing it. Maybe you're someone who's often late. Notice when you want to do one more thing before you leave the house, and don't do it.

Don't be too hard on yourself as you practise stopping. Our compulsions have very big muscles – they are designed to smash through any obstacles to get to the object of our desire. They think they are helping us. Sometimes we will notice we're entranced, and then will just go ahead and fetch the ice-cream or check Facebook anyway. Continuing to notice our behaviour without judging it, however, will work wonders. It's the drip drip drip of water onto a block of salt – without realising it, we are wearing away at the strength our compulsions, and allowing the possibility for different choices. We can notice, and we can practise stopping.

If you are very attached to your compulsion, whatever it is, then I would suggest that you spend some time trying to get as honest as you can about how it's affecting you. Is it affecting your health, relationships, work, mood or finances? How? What have you lost? How might your life look without it? What would your loved ones say about it? Would you be brave enough to ask them? How much pain are you in? Honestly answering this question may lead you to the first of the Twelve Steps, where we admit that we are powerless over our compulsion, and that our lives have become unmanageable. You may not believe me, but truly reaching this step is a wonderful thing, because it gives us a huge opportunity we didn't have before – to stop doing what hasn't been working, to seek help, and to see our life change beyond recognition. If you're nearly there, go to a 12 Step meeting, see your doctor, book a therapy session, confess to a friend, or do whatever you need to do to start your recovery. And keep doing it, one day at a time. You don't need to be alone. The alternative to compulsion is always freedom. There is always hope.

Questions for reflection

What feelings came up as you read this chapter?

Do you recognise times when it feels like you can't stop?

What are your favourite urges and compulsions? Which ones cause the most havoc?

When are you more likely to experience urges and compulsions?

If you stopped doing something you feel you couldn't stop, what might your life look like?

What small thing could you practise stopping?

If you want to tackle a larger addiction or compulsion, where might you start? What help could you ask for?

Are there different bits of you that you haven't been listening to?

When are you most free?

How could you increase your freedom today?

Let go of clinging

> *Epictetus concludes that if one practices being indifferent to one's possessions, one will not be angry at those who snatch them away, and in this way one will become 'invincible.'*
> ~ Anna Wierzbicka

I am currently on retreat with three writers I don't know, and earlier I went downstairs to make my lunch from the selection of food provided for us. I had seen four fat avocados in the fruit bowl earlier, and I was very much looking forward to a Buddha bowl made from one of these beauties, a dollop of houmus, the leftover brown rice from last night's meal, and the sweet baby tomatoes on the vine.

I assembled the rest of the meal and went to fetch an avocado... They weren't there. For a moment I could hardly believe it. There were four of us, and four avocados – surely they hadn't all been taken? They seemed like such nice women – how could they have taken all the avocados for themselves? I went back to look in the fruit bowl several times before admitting they were gone.

I felt sharp disappointment and a simmering resentment. The pain was caused by the attachment I'd formed to the avocados I'd seen, which were never mine in the first place. Someone else had enjoyed them. I had the rice, tomatoes, houmus, olives, cucumber and baby salad leaves, good olive oil, and fresh bread. There were also crisps, vegan pate, oatcakes, bananas, chocolate puddings…

We all become attached to all sorts of things – people, places, objects and ideas. This is inevitable and it brings us a good deal of comfort. Why the need for relinquishing? You might think that you'd quite like to hang onto your attachments, thank you very much. Surely they don't lead to much more grief than a lost avocado here or there. I asked my Dharma teacher once if I was allowed to hold onto any of my attachments – maybe just chocolate? He laughed and said, of course you can, if you don't want to be free.

If we choose to hold onto our attachment to chocolate, when we crave chocolate we are choosing chocolate over our freedom. We enter a state where the only thing in front of our eyes is chocolate or no-chocolate. Everything else disappears. Eating chocolate gives us temporary relief, but the satisfaction fades quickly as the sugar high fades. Not having chocolate when we desperately want it leaves us missing out on whatever else we could be doing or thinking or feeling, as our bodies and minds mobilise in one direction. We miss the myriad of riches the world has to offer us.

Wherever we would like to be free, we can practise letting go of our attachments or, more accurately, recognising that we never had any control over the thing we're attracted to in the first place. Aitken Roshi says that: "Renunciation is not getting rid of the things of this world, but accepting that they pass away." A travelling monk who's stayed for ten months in our biggest room with a claw-foot bath (he christened it 'the honeymoon suite') is about to go back on the road. He was asked if he'd miss the room when he's in his cold tent in the forest. He replied that every day he's been here, he's appreciated it as if it were the only day he had. He feels completely okay to let go of the comfort of the bath and to move on.

We think that when we relinquish stuff, we'll end up with less of it. What actually happens is the opposite. The Zen master Suzuki Roshi said: "Do not steal. When we think we do not possess something, then we want to steal. But actually everything in the world belongs to us, so there is no need to steal. For example, my glasses. They are just glasses. They do not belong to me or you, or they belong to all of us. But you know about my tired old eyes, and so you let me use them." Like the chocolate, letting go of what we think we need opens us up to receiving infinitely more.

I finished my lunch, did some more writing, and later went down to make a cup of tea, Someone had crossed out 'avocados' on the list I'd made of food that needed restocking and written 'Sue has put them in a drawer to ripen'. I opened the drawer: there they all were, still too hard to eat, but being taken care of by Sue for us all. When I read the note, I laughed out loud. The universe was reminding me, yet again, that I didn't need to worry about not having enough of anything. That I would always be provided for, regardless of what I thought I did or didn't need.

My favourite mug splashed with bright orange orchids visited me for five years, and then it was smashed. My ex-partner cooked me exquisite meals, made me laugh, and taught me most of what I know about relationships, and then we parted. The money from my best-selling novel bought a posh greenhouse and converted a garage in the house we soon (unexpectedly) moved out of. Avocados come, and avocados go. It is in our nature to cling, but whenever we can loosen our grip and let go, we are blessed.

> *Only one thing*
> *made him happy*
> *and now that*
> *it was gone*
> *everything*
> *made him happy.*
> *~ Leonard Cohen*

Questions for reflection

What objects are you most attached to? Your house or car? Your clothes? Your family heirlooms? Your money?

What work or worry is involved in maintaining these objects?

Do you carry around any fear about losing these objects? What would happen if you lost them? How heavy is this fear?

Where are your attachments in your relationships? How do you need people to be in order to be okay?

What do you cling to most tightly? Why?

What would you like to relinquish? (You don't have to give the object away, just the desperate need to keep the object – of course, once you've let go of the desperate need, it won't matter if it does go!)

What one attachment is keeping you from enjoying the other things that are available to you in your life?

Savour solitude

> *I feel the same way about solitude as some people feel about the blessing of the church. It's the light of grace for me. I never close my door behind me without the awareness that I am carrying out an act of mercy toward myself.* ~ Peter Høeg

My name is Satya and I am codependent. This is what I say at the start of a group I attend, and it is true: I sometimes get into hopeless tangles with other people, mistaking them for my Higher Power and trying to please them, or deciding I'm their Higher Power and trying to change them. I don't think I'm that unusual, actually. Some of us are experts at manipulating, others tend to isolate or to use passive aggression, but we all have our preferred ways of trying to feel safe around other people and these strategies sometimes get us into trouble.

When I am on my own I can begin to sort through some of these tangles, like teasing out the knots in our old cat's fur. It's very difficult to see a tangle clearly when we're inside it. Solitude gives me a space where I can step back and begin to see what I'm up to without getting more tangled. It's where I work out where I end and where others begin. It's where I stop blaming others and start owning the things I've been trying to get rid of.

As well as helping me deal with other people, being alone also helps me to become more intimate with myself, with the world, and with the Buddha. Ram Dass says that "The quieter you become, the more you can hear." I find that the best wisdom is often spoken very quietly, in amongst the louder clamouring of the marketplace and of our own greed, hate and delusion. Wisdom whispers, 'You really don't like that new person you're dating'. It says, 'You're feeling really sad about your sister moving away'. It asks, 'You used to love walking in the woods – why don't you do that any more?'

I do sometimes find it hard to be alone. With no distractions, the feelings that I've been squishing down will often seize their opportunity and erupt. I feel sad, confused, jittery, frustrated or hopeless, often for no reason I can discern. It sucks. We honour our solitude when we sit alongside ourselves quietly and ask ourselves how we're doing, even if we'd rather be out playing crazy golf, or doing anything. We write in our journal or go on walks. We run ourselves hot baths and cry if we want to. We know that, if we squish it all back down again, it'll only ambush us the next time we close the door behind us. We might even manage to welcome the uncomfortable feelings as Rumi suggests in his poem The Guest House, curious about what our visitors might have to say.

When my awkward visitors have had their say and quieted down, I reach a depth of peace when I'm alone that's very difficult in the presence of others. It's just me and the birds, me and the trees, me and the Buddha. I feel nourished and inspired, and energised to go out and face the world again. Sweet solitude can be a true act of mercy. May you find the same.

Questions for reflection

How is it for you to be alone?

How often do you spend time alone?

Where are your favourite places to be alone?

What are the most difficult things about being alone for you? How could you lean into them a little further to investigate?

When you're alone, what visitors from your psyche tend to come and knock on your door? Do you make them feel welcome? What are you afraid might happen if you invite them in?

When you are alone, how is it to reflect on your relationships? Your work? Your creativity? The balance in your daily life?

If it's difficult for you to find alone-time, how could you squeeze a little in? Could you get up a little early or share childcare with a friend? What support would you need from others? What resistance do you meet in yourself or in others?

Do you ever appreciate the sweetness of solitude? If not, what gets in the way?

Do you admire anyone who regularly spends time alone? What do they do when they are alone? How is it to observe them?

When can you next be alone?

Step towards fear

> *No one ever tells us to stop running away from fear... the advice we usually get is to sweeten it up, smooth it over, take a pill, or distract ourselves, but by all means make it go away.* ~ Pema Chödrön

In the Tibetan Buddhist tradition there is a story about a sage called Milarepa who returns from gathering firewood to find that his cave has been taken over by demons. He tries to chase them out, but they dodge him effortlessly. After a while he stops, exhausted, and as they sit there looking smug he expounds some of his best Dharma teachings to try and convert them to good. It has no effect on them whatsoever. Finally he surrenders and welcomes them, asking them what they have to teach him. As he bows to each demon in turn they disappear in a puff of smoke – all except the biggest nastiest demon, who looms at him slavering and growling. Milarepa moves even closer to this demon, putting his head right inside his mouth with its long sharp teeth. As he does this, the fiercest demon finally disappears.

Milarepa was able to look his biggest fear square in the eyes, and it rendered it powerless. It is the last thing we want to do. If we think there are monsters under the bed, we want to sleep in a different bed – and we certainly don't want to hang our heads down over the mattress and peer into the musty darkness. Unfortunately, when we refuse to look at them, monsters tend to grow rather than shrink. Like Milarepa's demons they take up more and more space in our lives, and we begin to rearrange our furniture or take long detours to avoid going near them. Before we know it, we've let them take over the whole bedroom.

We've been carrying our own distinctive set of fears around with us for a long time. We might be plagued by a fear of getting the sack or of our wife leaving us, we have miscellaneous phobias, we are afraid of illness or dying, or we have a dread of failing our children... We have probably already tried all sorts of things to keep these fears at bay – medication, distraction, elaborate avoidance, blame – anything! When we're ready to try something different, the first thing we need to do is to surrender. At this point in the story, Milarepa realises that none of his previous energetic strategies have worked, and that the demons are here to stay. A calm descends. Now we can begin.

We begin by taking a very small step towards one of our fears. We don't tackle them all at once, and we don't rush or force ourselves. Maybe we take a friend with us who can hold our hand, or maybe we take our fears into therapy or into nature. Maybe the first step is hardly a step forwards at all, but we manage to stay where we are for two seconds before running away again. There's no point in frightening ourselves further – Milarepa only put his head in the demon's mouth when he was ready. What you will discover is, fear is 'false evidence appearing real'. The biggest fear we have is of fear itself. Yes, difficult stuff will happen, and yes, it will feel horrible, but we will come through it, and we will survive.

I quoted Teresa of Avila earlier, who said: "Let nothing disturb you. Let nothing frighten you. Everything passes away except God." I invite you to lean into this sense of fearlessness she was speaking about. In order to feel truly safe, we need to leave the false security of our duvets. We need to move towards the edge of our beds, bit by bit, and poke our heads down over the edge of the mattress until we can see Under The Bed. We need to breathe slowly and speak encouragingly to ourselves as our eyes adjust to the darkness...

Questions for reflection

What are you afraid of? Make a (long) list.

How do these fears affect you? What do they stop you from doing?

How would life be if you could loosen the grip of some of these fears?

Take one fear at a time. What would help you to take a very small step towards this fear?

How can you be kind to yourself as you take this step? Who can you ask for help?

How has it been when you've stepped towards fear in the past?

Can you take a step towards fear today?

If in doubt, wait

Patience is also a form of action. ~ Auguste Rodin

A long time ago I started attending a 12 step group for people affected by someone else's drinking. I had completely exhausted my own resources. I was in torment over my relationship with my then-partner, who was drinking heavily. We had been together a decade, and I loved him, but it was very painful to watch him harm himself, and there were lots of confusing tangles in the relationship. In the 12 step group I was bombarded with new information, and advice from the other members and in the literature I read. I filtered everything I heard and read through the same desperate question – should I stay with him or should I leave?

Something I read and heard over and over again was, if you're in doubt about whether or not to leave your relationship, don't leave just yet and keep 'working the programme'. We were told to do what we needed to do in order to keep ourselves safe, and then refrain from making any big decisions. I didn't know what was good for me any more, and so I followed this advice. I attended weekly groups where I heard other people speaking about their own experiences with alcoholism, I read the literature, and I experimented with detaching with love. I also learnt a great deal about my own codependency – how I used manipulation, feeling superior, colluding and denial to keep the dysfunctional dynamic going. I was officially 'in recovery', and I began to heal.

I continued to agonise about what I should do, but I didn't make any decisions about my relationship until about a year into my recovery. I'd gone to visit my single friend Jenny in London. As I watched her moving around her lovely little flat, making tea for me and talking about her daily life, I realised that it would be possible for me to be single. The time was finally ripe. I still loved my partner, and I left him that week, with love, deep sadness, and a feeling of complete 'rightness'.

If in doubt, wait. We can apply this in complex situations like the ending of a relationship or a career, and we can also apply it in miniature. Sometimes when I'm with a psychotherapy client I will notice a pattern or a link and I have the urge to say something, but I hesitate. Maybe they're in their flow, or I'm not sure I'm correct, or it may be that I'm afraid it might be too much for them to hear. When this happens I hold my tongue and trust that, if it's important, it will come up again. To borrow an illuminating phrase from a child-centred psychotherapeutic approach, I 'wait, watch, and wonder'. Sometimes the impulse comes up again and I mention it to the client, and sometimes whatever-it-is drifts away.

Of course, some of us need to go left a bit, and some of us need to go right a bit. If you are someone who uses procrastination as a way of avoiding decisions, watching and waiting might not be the best advice for you. Sometimes we just need to step off the top of the hundred foot pole, trusting that there is no such thing as a 'perfect' decision and that any action can sometimes be better than staying stuck in inaction. How do we know the difference? The trick is to pay attention to the quality of the waiting. If our waiting feels alive – if we have thoughts and feelings moving through us, and new insights emerge over time – then we are still ripening and it may be premature to make a decision or to speak. If we feel deadened, closed off, it may be that we are using the waiting as a defence, to avoid facing something we don't want to face.

Sometimes we only need to pause for the length of a deep breath before we act – giving ourselves a little space to check in with ourselves. Sometimes, like my decision to leave a relationship, we might need to wait a year or many years. If I'd left my partner before the end of that year, as many of my friends were advising me to do, I wouldn't have been ready to face life alone. My ambivalence and my own unhealthy tendencies would have travelled with me, putting me in danger of going back, or of starting another relationship with a similar dynamic. By the time I left, I was finished – and within a few months I met my future husband.

Waiting is hard. Not-knowing nags at us to choose a direction – any direction – to relieve the tension. The gold is in turning neither left nor right. When we practise waiting we sit down, we make ourselves as comfortable as we can, and observe our koan in process. Let the ocean of love and light ripen you and know that, when the time is right, the decision will be as simple as easing a ripe plum from a tree.

Questions for reflection

What dilemmas are you currently struggling with? Do you feel an urge to make a decision?

How would it be to put off making a decision whilst you do? What do you need to do to start healing?

What is your version of recovery – the things you can do to start healing yourself and learning about yourself while you're waiting?

How could you make yourself more comfortable as you wait?

How is it for you to wait? What feelings come up?

Do you know anyone who takes their time with decisions and with the things they say?

What does impatience look like for you?

Are there areas in your life where you need to take some action rather than waiting further?

How could you reframe a period of waiting as a gift to yourself?

Could you give yourself permission right now to wait a little longer before you make a particular decision?

Write things right

Pain told accurately transmutes to grace. Writing is the way I meditate. ~ Sage Cohen

This morning I wrote in my journal, as I often do. I wrote about a fraught dream I had last night where I saw a dead man at the bottom of a deep pit. I wrote about the glossy blackbird I could see hopping about on the lawn. I wrote about my tasks for today. I wrote about a grey loneliness that lies underneath my urges to check Facebook.

There is great power in articulating our experience. We can do this out loud, by speaking with friends or a therapist, but other people aren't always available to us, especially in the middle of the night. My journal is always available, and it is always listening.

Our unspoken and unwritten thoughts can have a tendency to get stuck on repeat like a scratched record. We return to the same itch, maybe feeling a moment's relief but then finding ourselves back there again before long. We tend to repeat ourselves (both in our heads and to other people) because what we are saying hasn't been properly heard or understood. We have a yearning that hasn't been met, and we keep telling our story in the hope that someone will recognise it, even if we don't know what we're doing or what we need. How do we get closer to this yearning?

When we get something out onto paper, instead of being completely caught up in our experience, there is a part of us which becomes a witness and reads what we have written. This witness part has the quality of looking in on someone else and feeling curious about their behaviour. Even a slight step back may be enough to give us a different perspective on what we're writing about. 'Oh, I'm/she's writing about him again – I wonder why he triggers me/her so much?' Or, 'when I/she writes that, I/she sounds like a sad little girl...' In witnessing our written-down thoughts, we are given an opportunity to peel back a layer of our experience and to see what's underneath more clearly.

The effort of translating our experience into the right words can also facilitate the process of both becoming clearer and of feeling more empathetic towards ourselves. Is it that we feel betrayed, or is 'tricked' a better word? How do we feel in our stomach when we encounter our colleague? We might start with 'I feel rubbish' and then wonder, what does rubbish feel like to me? What is happening in my body? What happens when I take a deep breath? What memory floats up from the depths? We are seeing ourselves in the mirror of the page, and learning as we go.

Sometimes we learn more about ourselves and about the situation we're in when we write in the form of a dialogue. You can imagine that you are talking to yourself, or maybe you want a conversation with your Higher Power or the angels. Start with a question – 'Why am I feeling so tired?' – and then write down the answer that comes. Then ask another question or say something else. Don't worry about whether it's really the angels talking to you or not – just stay open and keep talking. I find that unexpected material often emerges when I write in this way, and that I'm more likely to receive some new insights than when I'm just 'talking to myself'.

You could also try a practice like Morning Pages, prescribed for blocked artists by Julia Cameron, where we write three pages of long-hand stream-of-consciousness writing on waking every day. This takes about twenty minutes. You write down whatever comes out of your pen – a record of your dreams, your hopes and fears for the day, memories, complaining, praising, or even the same phrase over and over. I've had long periods of doing daily Morning Pages in the past and it is a powerful and fertile practice – Ruth, the protagonist of my first novel, first appeared in my Pages, and I also used them to write endlessly about all my favourite neuroses – some of them even improved slightly as a result!

As well as helping us to get clearer about what's going on inside us, writing also helps us to pay attention to the world around us, as we do when we write *small stones*. This mindful writing is a form of meditation. As we scan our environment and focus in on something we'd like to make a record of, we first open our hearts and minds, letting more information in, and then sharpen our senses, zoning in on details and being as specific as we can. Not blue, but lapis lazuli. Not cobwebs, but trembling strands of dark grey spider-silk.

It is a good practice to consciously expand the boundaries of what we are aware of, as we often exclude information which is potentially helpful to us. Writing helps us to expand our known territory in many dimensions – spiritually, emotionally, in our thinking, and in our physical experience of the world. We are always asking ourselves, what is new here? What haven't I noticed? What have I been trying to ignore? What is the Universe trying to tell me?

Writing also connects us to gratitude. After I write this sentence I pause, with the intention of writing a handful of *small stones*. I look up from my screen. The light shines on the creases in the robe of my silver Buddha on the windowsill, and there is the promise of my mug of hot golden tea, breathing out steam. The triangular flame on my writing candle is steady, the tip of it reminding me of the tip of my tongue, and it lights the way for me as I write. My chair is solid underneath me. My intricately lobed lungs are relaxing and squeezing all the time, without me asking them to. So many wonderful things come forwards when I stop and look. Gratitude flows into me.

Maybe you're skipping through this chapter, thinking that you're not any good at writing. You're not alone in doubting your ability to write. I've been writing professionally for many years and I still feel afraid of the white page. I still have voices that tell me I'm a dreadful writer – how could I have the audacity to think that people would want to read my books? Writing is an act of creation and all acts of creation take courage. We have to listen to our doubts, acknowledge them, and then sit down and start writing anyway.

I'd also like to remind you that your journal doesn't care whether you get your spelling or grammar right. It doesn't care if you use long words or short ones. It just wants to hear how you are. It's the same with *small stones* or other forms of creative writing. What's at the heart of writing isn't the finished product or any praise you might receive from others, but the process of searching for the words and translating experience into sentences. It may be that you enjoy the results of your writing as a happy by-product, but try not to get too seduced by that. Keep stretching and strengthening your observation and articulation muscles and the rest will look after itself.

Writing is always about making a connection with an Other, whether this Other is an objective view of our own self or the tiny vivid blue flowers waving outside my window. It creates a gateway between our tight, closed-down selves and the wider world. It helps the good stuff to get in, and the dark stuff to sink away into the earth. It's wonderful that we leave something behind when we write, like making patterns with leaves on the lawn, but we remember that the wind will come and blow them away at some point anyway. We take pleasure in the arranging, and we open ourselves up to learning about ourselves and about the world. We keep writing. Sometimes, we might even receive the gift of grace.

Questions for reflection

How do you currently use writing in your life?

Have you ever played with creative writing? Would you like to? What is stopping you?

Have you ever kept a journal? How did you/do you use it? Would you like to start using one, or visiting it more regularly?

Would you like to try writing *small stones* or Morning Pages? When will you start?

Have you ever written letters to people as a way of processing emotion? Who might you want to write a letter to? Don't feel you need to give it to them – the writing is the important bit.

What do you long to write?

What do the voices in your head tell you about how you write? What might happen if you thanked them for their input and then carried on anyway?

Do you want some extra support for your writing – a writing group, or an online course, or a writing friend who you arrange to meet once a month?

How can you make more space for writing in your life?

Would you like to write a *small stone* right now?

Make vows

> *Innumerable are sentient beings, we vow to save them all*
> *Inexhaustible are deluded passions, we vow to transform them all*
> *Immeasurable are the Dharma teachings, we vow to master them all*
> *Infinite is the Buddha's way, we vow to fulfill it completely*
> ~ Bodhisattva Vows

I love these words, which we chant regularly as a part of our Buddhist services. They seem to perfectly encapsulate the impossibility of keeping vows. Even less ambitious vows such as avoiding gossip or even keeping the house-plants watered are impossible to keep 100% of the time. Reciting the Bodhisattva Vows often brings a wry smile to my face, as I imagine myself trying to save innumerable beings, transform inexhaustible passions and master immeasurable teachings. Trying and (spectacularly) failing.

And yet. There is also a beauty in making vows. Even the word has a generous full-bellied sound, a certain gravitas. What are vows? Vows give us a direction to sail towards. They let us know whether we need to turn left a bit or right a bit. They stand ahead of us like a beacon, inspiring us and encouraging us forwards. Lighting the way.

When I became ordained as a Buddhist Priest I took 156 vows as a part of the Ordination ceremony. I don't know these all off by heart, but I know that they guide me and help hold me to account when I take unskilful actions. They are like a kindly tap on my shoulder – 'I see that you have put a small tip in the bowl as you are feeling anxious about money. Don't worry, you can be more generous.' 'You just put the potato peelings in the rubbish and not in the compost bin. It'd be kinder to the environment if you just took a minute to move them.'

This list of vows show me when there is a gap between my behaviour and the behaviour of an enlightened being. When I notice this gap, sometimes I find that I can take a step towards more ethical behaviour (moving the potato peelings), and sometimes I can't (continuing to gossip with a friend despite knowing I shouldn't). That's okay. Vows are not intended to become sticks that you beat yourself with. First of all, as the Bodhisattva Vows acknowledge, as fallible human beings we are utterly inadequate to the task of 'completing' or 'perfecting' our vows. Secondly, sticks are not helpful tools to aid spiritual growth. Unless they are kyōsaku sticks, maybe... (hitting sticks that are judiciously deployed to wake meditators up in both senses of the word in Zen temples). The problem with sticks is that they hurt, and when we hurt our muscles tense up and we get frightened of being hit again. Being afraid is never a good medium for growing change.

When we work with vows, we are learning to find the middle way between overly high and unrealistic expectations of ourselves on the one hand, and half-heartedness and excuses on the other hand. We keep our eye on the vow, as a tightrope walker will fix their gaze on a single spot ahead of them, and step forwards one little step at a time. When we fall off (don't worry, there are big trampolines to catch us) we feel appropriate contrition, make amends if appropriate, and then get back up on the rope and carry on.

I was given my 156 vows as a part of my ordination, and I was also asked to write a personal vow which I read out as part of my ceremony. Creating this vow from scratch has given it an extra power. It is designed both to acknowledge my weaknesses, and to make the most of my strengths. I used language that resonates with me and that inspires me. The vow I wrote was "May I let go into Amitabha's grace and follow the light with humility, strength and love." What is your personal vow? It might be "May I be more patient with my children and forgiving of myself", or "Help me to learn every day" or "I vow to reduce the suffering of animals". Don't rush it – spend time with it and let it reveal itself to you.

Once you've written your vow or vows, a simple ceremony will help you to activate it. This could be done either alone or with witnesses. Light a candle and read your vow out loud, maybe asking the Universe or your Higher Power to help you. Place it somewhere you can see it and be reminded of it – in the front of your journal, in your wallet, or by your computer. Learn it by heart, and see it not as a stick to beat yourself with, but as a beautiful light to guide you forwards.

Innumerable are sentient beings. We vow to save them all.

Questions for reflection

What vows have you already taken? Wedding vows? Were you a member of the Guides or Scouts? Have you made any promises to your friends or your families?

Have you made any vows to yourself? Have they ever been helpful?

What has been your experience of vows in the past? Do you feel inspired by them? What happens when you break them?

Are you realistic about what you are generally capable of? Do your expectations of yourself tend to be too high or too low? What consequences ensue?

Can you see the beauty of vows or do you just see them as sticks?

Can you see how vows can act as a guiding light?

Are there any vows that you feel called to take?

Simplify

> *I wish I might emphasize how a life becomes simplified when dominated by faithfulness to a few concerns. Too many of us have too many irons in the fire.* ~ Thomas R Kelly

My life has two modes. In the first, on waking I dive into my phone to see who has contacted me in the night. When I start up my computer I check various social media sites, and flick between them and whatever else I'm working on. I come in from the garden just to check my email. When reading I cradle my phone to the right of my open book, and flick between the page and the screen. My brain is scattered like light through a crystal, and my cogs whir a little too fast. In the second mode, I check my email and the internet once a day, after midday. Time stretches out around me like a cat in a patch of sun.

What have you done so far today? How many different tasks are calling for your attention? How many people are dependent on you in some way? How many emails have you received? What does your diary look like over the coming week or year? What would happen if you got sick and needed a month off? Where are the spaces where you can breathe?

Most of us feel pulled in different directions, like a dog let off its leash onto a beach full of fascinating smells. There can be advantages to living like this – we 'get lots done', and we feel productive or useful as a result. We might get a nice buzzy feeling from the stimulation, the variety and the adrenaline as we keep all our balls in the air. It may help us to avoid feeling our feelings as we fill every being-space with doing.

There is also a list of disadvantages. We never have the time to do anything properly and this leaves us disappointed and dissatisfied. As tasks build up we feel overwhelmed or panicky, and this stress leaves us bad-tempered or unwell. We don't spend enough time on our heart-work - the creative tasks that are important to us - or on the relationships we want to foster, or on savouring solitude.

We know that simplifying our lives would probably make us feel better. We could enjoy leisurely breakfasts at the weekend, time reading our new novel, or messing about with our children in the local park. We would feel less stretched and less stressed. Why is it is so difficult to put into practice?

When I examine my own tendency towards complication, I see that it is fuelled by many things, including the greediness of not wanting to miss out, a desire for praise, feeling flattered when people ask me to do things, and an anxiety about empty spaces. I work hard to create space, quitting committees and putting new projects on pause, and then find myself filling it all back in before I've had a chance to savour it. Others might feel pressured by their families, society or financial responsibilities to shove more into their days, they might have bullying internal voices that say things like 'don't be so lazy', or they might simply be doing what their parents always did.

I am inspired to move towards the direction of simplicity by several things - mostly, the importance of prioritising heart-work like my writing and spiritual contemplative study. I won't produce fresh writing or thinking if I squeeze it into twenty minutes before rushing out to a meeting – I need regular hours, longer periods every so often, and little spaces around the edges of the rest of my life to allow for the necessary composting. It also helps to practise saying no and delegating, go on retreats, and do some practical things like limiting the number of appointments I have each day or blocking out regular time in my diary to write and to review my workload. What helps you?

Thoreau reminds us that "Our life is frittered away by detail" if we don't keep things simple. This frittering away matters – we don't have the option to live portions of our life again. Those hours you spent watching videos of people falling over will never be returned to you. I hope that you don't need to become ill or witness the death of someone close to you before you reappraise the way you currently live your life. I invite you to start sucking the juice from every day, starting today. Get out your diary and your pruning shears, and begin some judicious clipping. Enjoy watching your blowsy sweet-scented roses bloom.

Questions for reflection

How complicated is your life right now?

Do you know what your heart-work is? What are your priorities? Do you currently feel you have enough time to do the things that are important to you?

How often do you feel overwhelmed by your 'to do' list?

Why do you tend towards busyness?

Remember a time in your life when things were simpler. What was different about your everyday life?

Do you know anyone currently living a simpler life? What do you like about their life? What inspires you?

What supports you to keep an eye on how complicated your life is getting?

Whose help do you need to make some changes towards simplification?

If you woke up to an 'empty' day tomorrow, how would that be? Would you have any fears? What would you most look forward to?

Could you set aside a day a week (like a Sabbath) where you practice simplicity, maybe not watching television or not organising any appointments?

How could you begin to simplify your life right now?

Find faith

> *At long last I saw, I felt, I believed. Scales of pride and prejudice fell from my eyes. A new world came into view.* ~ The Big Book of Alcoholics Anonymous

When I first joined my 12 step programme, I noticed that the people in the group I most admired were also the ones who talked about their Higher Power. They also used the G word, seemingly interchangeably. At this time I had a severe allergic reaction to the word God, and the F word, faith. I associated spirituality with weirdness and weakness – these people must be religious crack-pots, dependent on silly stories from thousands of years ago, morally immature, prone to evangelising...

As time went on I grew to like and trust these people, particularly my sponsor. One day I heard the acrostic 'Good Orderly Direction' as an alternative to the word God. I wasn't sure if 'orderly' was the best way of describing Universe's process – it looked pretty chaotic to me! I did, however, like the idea that there may be something unfolding that we don't fully understand, and that we can tentatively describe this unfolding as heading in a good direction. It chimed with my experience of what happens in therapy, as my clients moved inexorably towards health, and how I saw the earth's ecosystem as creating ever more complex, beautiful life.

My sponsor told me that she also used to have a huge reaction to the word God. Over time she'd been able to read the word 'God' as a short-hand for her own concept of a Higher Power. This opened her mind and allowed her to receive all kinds of wisdom from writings and teachings she would have dismissed before. Regardless of what tradition they came from, she could test the teachings out against her own experience and see if they were helpful to her. She then encouraged me to find myself a Higher Power, something I didn't have at the time. She said it didn't matter what it was, she told me about someone who'd chosen the radiator as their Higher Power. The important bit was beginning to trust that there was something outside of me that I could rely on – a benign process, a collective wisdom, 'Love' – however I wanted to see it.

I started by using the 12 step group as my Higher Power, treating it as if it might have more wisdom than I had. I was pretty sceptical. I'd always been the kind of person who relied on my own wisdom above anyone else's, and so imagining that the group might know more than I did was a big step! I opened my mind to receiving something new from the group, and to my surprise it happened week after week. I witnessed the group self-regulating without my intervention, and I began to relax and lean into it. Sometimes the person I least expected to would share a story that gave me the exact insight I needed. The group nourished me, and held me when I felt vulnerable.

Encouraged, I invented myself a Higher Power called Bob. Sometimes I talked to him before I went to sleep, feeling foolish and amused at myself. I found that talking to Bob about things that were difficult seemed to help me, especially when I 'handed them over' for him to deal with. I even started asking him for help... Who was this person I was turning into? I continued to feel sceptical, but buoyed up by relief, fresh insights and glimpses of deep consolation, I continued. It eventually led me to Buddhism and to running the temple I run now.

You might already have a relationship with a Higher Power. If your HP is kind, patient and forgiving, that's wonderful – you can continue to do the things that help you to connect more fully with this HP. If your HP isn't these things, then it may be worth reconsidering. Where did your conceptualisation of your HP come from? Was it your direct experience? We sometimes get our Higher Powers mixed up with the worst of our parents, or we hold onto ideas from the religion we grew up with. Experiment with imagining a different form of your HP and see how this chimes with your experience of the world. This isn't an easy process – our ideas of God, especially if they are tied up with our potential guilt or salvation or our experiences around authority, can be difficult to untangle and approach afresh.

If the idea of having faith in a Higher Power is new to you, I would like to suggest that you invent one as I did, just as an experiment, and see where it takes you. Write a list of the characteristics you would like your Higher Power to have, and then start imagining them there, keeping an eye on you and being there for you to lean into. You might say the Serenity Prayer every morning to summon them, or light a candle and sit quietly for five minutes. You might even feel called to do some reading about various spiritual traditions, or sit quietly in a Cathedral, or go on a walk and make an offering to the Gods of

Nature. Follow your curiosity, take it slowly, persevere through your scepticism, and enjoy!

Step 11 of the Twelve Steps is about 'improving our conscious contact with God as we understood God', and it is my favourite step. It is like making time to hang out with that lovely friend you haven't seen for ages, and who always leaves you feeling good about yourself. We need to find our own ways of doing this. Some of my ways include doing Buddhist practice on my own or with others, spending time alone in nature, writing letters to Amida Buddha, reading spiritual books, lighting a candle before I start writing, going on retreat, spending time with people who have a deep sense of their own faith and buying Buddha statues. Some would say too many statues, but I hold that there's no such thing as too many... Living in a Buddhist temple does help me with Step 11, but even here I need to frequently remind myself of the benefits of fostering faith. Like any good relationship, our relationship with our Higher Power flourishes when we remember to buy her flowers, share our vulnerability with her, and most of all listen to what she has to say.

Now that I have an experience of faith myself, I can see that people of faith have a special quality to them, like a golden aura. Lin-Chi says that "It's because you don't have enough faith that you rush around moment by moment looking for something." These people don't need to rush around because they have a deep feeling that things will be okay, even when they're not okay. I intuited this quality when I first met my Buddhist teacher Dharmavidya, and I remember experiencing it in others – a Christian colleague when I was doing my therapy training, and a school friend's mum. I find that people of faith have a steady quality to them. They are realistic about the horrors of life, but they have open hearts and deep courage, and they hold onto a fierce hope that everything will turn out okay even when it's not okay. If we spend time around these people, their faith will rub off on us.

In my experience, there is something I lean into which isn't me. When I began to do this, it changed my life. Leaning into (in my case) the Buddha underpins everything that I do. If I hadn't found this faith, I wouldn't have this wonderful life I have now – my good marriage, this beautiful temple, my precious sangha, and my relationship with the Buddha which always steadies me. There is still suffering – the Buddha is clear when he says that we can't avoid that – but with our Higher Power beside us we can face this suffering with nobility and remain open to the millions of gifts that stream into our lives without ceasing.

Questions for reflection

What feelings move through you as you read this chapter?

Do you have faith? In what?

How do you feel when you read the words God or Faith? What experiences are behind these feelings?

Can you remember any times when having faith helped you?

What does it feel like to lean into faith?

How much faith do you have in your own capabilities or capacity? When or where does this fail you?

Are you inspired by anyone you know who seems to have faith, whether in a religion or in the goodness of humanity or in nature?

What spiritual practices do you enjoy? How could you find more space for these practices?

How could you spend more time with your Higher Power? How could you rely on them more?

What first step might you take towards either beginning or improving your relationship with your Higher Power?

Open your heart

All the windows of my heart I open to the day.
~ John Greenleaf Whittier

In my Buddhist tradition, our main practice is to say the name of Amida Buddha as a way of connecting to his infinite love and light. My first solitary retreat was a chanting retreat, and I spent it in a small hut in the garden of a temple in London. I spent four days chanting continuously from the moment I woke up to the moment I slid into sleep. Every day Acharya Modgala would bring me my food on a tray, always beautifully prepared, and check in with me to make sure I hadn't come unstuck.

On the third day, sometime in the afternoon, I was lying on my bed chanting when something happened to me. It was as if layers were being peeled away from around my heart, one by one – shoof! Shoof! Shoof! I felt a deep tenderness and connection with the world, and a deep gratitude to the simple hut that was sheltering me, the beauty of the garden around me, and the kindness in Modgala's carefully prepared meals. Once I left the retreat I settled back into my everyday life and the golden glow wore off, but those protective layers didn't regrow, and I was left with a tenderness that I can feel right now as I remember that afternoon. When our hearts have been opened, it changes us.

How can we open our hearts? We can't prise them open. Our hearts are like peonies; they hide in tight spherical buds until the sun warms them sufficiently and they burst out into extravagant frills. We have to be patient with our hearts. We have to coax them open by making safe spaces and by offering them understanding. They have been hurt many times in the past, and they are understandably wary. We need to show them over time that they can risk opening again.

One of my favourite pieces of liturgy in our tradition is The Prayer of All Lineages. It is a verse thanking a long list of previous Buddhist teachers from all the different Buddhist traditions for all the wisdom we've received from them. Each of the verses starts with the words, 'I open my heart to you'. I open my heart to you, Buddha Shakyamuni. I open my heart to you, foremost disciples. I open my heart to you, gurus of the Lotus lineage. It finishes:

> *From the hearts of all the Holy Beings*
> *Streams of light and amrita flow down*
> *Granting blessings and purifying.*

If we can open our hearts, we will be the recipients of infinite streams of light and nectar, blessing and purifying us. This is the promise made by the verse, and I believe it.

Questions for reflection

Where is your heart open?

Where is your heart closed?

Why have parts of your heart closed themselves down or shut themselves off? How were these parts wounded? How do they still hurt?

What fear do you have about opening your heart again?

What attention could you give to your heart to help heal it?

What have you received in the past when your heart has been open?

Who or what would you like to open your heart to?

What helps you to open your heart?

Could you allow it to open up a fraction right now?

Choose joy

> *When the eye is unobstructed, the result is sight. When the ear is unobstructed, the result is hearing. When the mouth is unobstructed, the result is taste. When the mind is unobstructed, the result is truth. And when the heart is unobstructed, the result is joy and love.*
> *~ Anthony de Mello*

Last year I bought some long stripy rainbow socks. Whenever I put them on, they made me happy. I wore them on a trip to my young nieces, hidden under my long red skirt, and they received rave reviews - when I got home I found some miniature versions online and put them in the post. My nieces were overjoyed, and that made me happy too.

Granted, rainbow socks are a very small thing when held up against the horrors inside and outside of us. The world groans with great suffering - poverty, earthquakes, cancer, terrorism - never mind the everyday suffering we all endure. We may feel undeserving of brightness, when so many of our fellow human beings are struggling. I think that the existence of these huge shadows give us an even better reason to search out the pools of light. What else can we do? And if we can find the light, especially when we are weighted with our own darkness, it will reflect in our faces and others will see that it is possible.

Tiny pockets of joy do add up. What works for you? Crooning to your dog or luxuriating in a rose-scented glittery-bath-bomb bath? Planting a bright red cyclamen, or going to a coffee shop on your own for a gingerbread soy latte? Putting time aside to write or paint? Helping out at your local school? Sending your great aunt a hand-written letter? Baking cupcakes with your children? Grabbing five minutes to promenade in the garden with your coffee trailing steam before the chaos of your day?

All sorts of things get in the way of joy, including our fearful grasping. There is a feast laid out in front of us, but we zoom in to the cherries – so glossy, so plump – we haven't had cherries for ages, if we could only have some of those cherries then we'd be happy. We forget that there is also home-baked walnut bread, and beetroot soup. We don't notice the new potatoes with good olive oil, or the spinach pie. Maybe our heart-block isn't that we're panicking about the cherries, but that we're obsessing about whether we upset our colleague. Maybe we're weighed down by unexpressed sadness, or anaesthetised by denial about how badly we're treating our sister. Heart-blocks are as infinitely unique as hearts.

Clearing the blockages from our heart is a long term project. We know we're making progress when we feel happy more easily and sad more easily – everything flows through smoothly, like an unblocked drain. In the meantime, little fragments of joy will find a way of sneaking in. Even in the middle of desolate grief, we can choose to taste the morsels of deliciousness that present themselves to us. The way our dog greets us when we come back into a room. The light reflecting off cobwebs. It doesn't mean that we're betraying the object of our grief or making light of it. When we look closely enough, all darkness contains light and all joy is bittersweet. The world would like us to enjoy it.

Joseph Campbell famously urged his students to 'follow their bliss'. I have found that I can trust what makes me feel good. Not a buzzy, compulsive pleasure but the good of wholesome nourishment. Following our bliss can help us to choose our careers, our partners and our friends. It can help us make decisions about what to do with our time, and which objects to keep and which to pass on. As Marie Kondo suggests in her wise books about tidying, when decluttering we hold objects to our hearts one by one and see if they bring a spark of joy. If they don't – however practical they might be, or however much we think they ought to make us happy, we pass them on. That almost-new pair of trousers deserve to live with someone who love them. The chipped glass you've kept for sentimental reasons is ready to be melted down and made into something new. Choosing fresh joy means letting go of old, stale joy.

Coming from a place of joy also helps us when we want to help others. The best helping isn't done self-consciously, from a place of 'ought' or pity. It also isn't motivated by a desire to be seen in a certain way, or to manipulate the person we're helping in some way. All of these motivations have fear mixed in with them, and they will lead to resentment in the giver and dissatisfaction for the receiver. Ideally, we give because we feel moved to do so when we connect with how much we have received. We are thank-full and we overflow with it.

Find the small things that make you happy and do them as often as you can. Unblock your heart and follow your bliss. If you embody joy, you will start radiating it out like a sun-warmed rock. People will come and stand near you to make the most of your glow. When you can see them receiving your warmth, it will warm you up even more. Joy is contagious.

Questions for reflection

What brings you joy? Make a list and make it as long as you can.

Which of these things are you in danger of missing when you are too busy or preoccupied?

Do you feel that you deserve to feel joy? Why?

What blocks you from joy?

Are you over-focussed on any one thing which is preventing you from enjoying the rest of the feast?

When do you feel happy? How does this affect how you treat others?

How could you choose joy today?

Pray

> *Prayer is not asking. Prayer is putting oneself in the hands of God, at His disposition, and listening to His voice in the depth of our hearts.*
> *~ Mother Teresa*

As I prepared to write this chapter, I read that several meta-studies of scientific experiments of prayer have found no or negligibly small positive effects when it is used to heal sick people. There may be plenty of anecdotal evidence for the power of prayer, but it seems we can't be sure that it makes any difference to people at all. Why, then, do people all over the world continue to do it? The Quakers resting in silence, the Buddhists and Muslims prostrating, the Christians singing, the grace we say over meals... What are we actually doing when we're praying?

Of course, I can't speak for everyone. Some people use prayer to ask for another car, to win the lottery, to ask for more than they need. Some people pray for terrible things to happen to other people. All I can do is speak about what prayer means to me, as an ex-atheist Buddhist Priest.

For me, prayer is about opening myself up to the good influence of the Buddhas. Prayer is about putting my ego aside and making a space for grace to enter. As Mother Teresa so beautifully puts it, in prayer we put ourselves in the hands of God.

I can't do this if I'm up on my ego-platform, directing things. I can only do this when I'm on my knees, either literally or metaphorically. I can only do this when I have reached a point where I need to ask for help – where I know that I can't do it on my own.

Praying is one of those words I used to have a negative visceral reaction to, along with words like grace, liturgy and faith. These same words now fill me with comfort and joy – I have reclaimed them, and built my own relationship with them. My suggestion to you is that praying will help you, regardless of whether you think it will or not. See it as an experiment. Humour me.

First, begin to develop some idea of what you are praying to. If you already have a concept of a Higher Power or a relationship with God, wonderful – as long as your God is kind, patient and forgiving. But if not, even if you're the most atheisty atheist there is, you can still choose something. Some people choose a particular group they trust, or humanity as a whole, or nature, or an abstract idea of the Good in the Universe. As I said I used to pray to an imaginary fellow called Bob, but now I'm a Buddhist Priest I've switched him for the Buddha. The important bit is that you don't choose you, or some part of yourself. 'You' is what we're trying to get away from.

Next, just start talking. You can do this out loud, or in your head, or in writing. Tell your Higher Power what you're fed up about, or what you'd like to change. Tell her what you feel grateful for, and who you'd like to send love to. Tell her your shameful secrets. Tell him about the things you can't bear. Tell him you don't think he exists or that you're furious with him. Tell your Higher Power everything.

If any problems come along that feel bigger than you can handle, hand them over to your Higher Power. Say, 'I'm going to let you deal with this', and imagine physically handing them over and letting go. Notice if you feel any small signs of relief. Keep an eye out for any different perspectives on the problem that present themselves to you over the coming days or months. These different perspectives might pop into your head, or they might come from something a friend or someone on the television says about something unrelated. If you continue to find yourself troubled by the problem, just hand it over again – as many times as you pick it up again. Continue taking action when you need to. Remember that you can't solve it alone, and it is possible that the world is wiser than you or can see more of the picture than you can.

Try these suggestions a few times a week for a month and see what happens. Trust that your Higher Power has your best interests at heart, and the best interests of the world at heart, even if sometimes it doesn't seem that way at all. Keep an open mind. Keep an ear open for anything your Higher Power might want to say or offer in return, but don't expect that you will get what you think you want – in praying we say what we want to say, we ask for help, we bow down before something that is bigger than us, and we surrender expectation.

After your experiments, if prayer seems weird and pointless to you and leaves you feeling worse, that's okay – stop doing it. If you don't know whether it's helping or not, carry on for a little bit longer. If it brings you some small crumbs of comfort and some little sparks of new insight, then savour these, and keep going.

> *I should not make any promises right now,*
> *But I know if you*
> *Pray*
> *Somewhere in this world –*
> *Something good will happen.*
> *~ Hafiz*

Questions for reflection

If you already pray, how do you use prayer? What do you pray for? What does it bring you? What does it bring the world?

How do you feel about surrendering and opening to something bigger and wiser than you?

What do you want to ask for help with?

Where do you feel the most alone?

How can you strip away the things you've been told or the things you've seen about prayer and find your own relationship with it?

What can you pray for right now?

Set boundaries

> *Through my own practice, I now see boundaries as being about stewardship, which means I have a responsibility for caring for this body and these mental and emotional states. If I'm a good steward, opportune conditions for both psychological development and spiritual freedom will arise, and I'll cause less suffering for myself and others. Good boundaries are not about "me" or my ego. Nor is there a feeling of "me" or "mine." Rather, there is harmony and possibility, or there is not.*
> ~ Phillip Moffitt

A fragment of a reality TV show from a decade ago has stuck in my mind. One of the popular, pretty girls was walking past one of the quirkier girls who was making herself a cup of coffee in the kitchen. Quirky offered Pretty a smile, and was met with a cool blank look. The interaction took only a few seconds but after Pretty had left, the camera caught Quirky silently re-enacting what had happened in an exaggerated form, clutching her heart and folding forwards as if she'd been stabbed by the cold look, her face scrunched up in pain. She repeated the motion a few times before turning back to her coffee.

This brief scene has stayed with me because it illustrates something many of us struggle with – identifying my feelings when I feel wounded by something someone else has said or done. I'm guessing that Quirky was learning how to identify and honour her reactions to other people's treatment of her. Rather than brushing this small incident off she paused to act out exaggerated pain to communicate with herself and get clear about what had happened. When she'd done this, and presumably also empathised with herself over her little wound, she was free to continue with her morning.

Why are we sometimes triggered like this by other people's actions? This arising of emotion – mostly pain or anger but sometimes confusion, sadness or something else – is often the first sign that one of our boundaries has been breached. By using the word 'breached' I don't mean to imply that the other person is intending to hurt us or disrespect us. Sometimes they are, in a more or a less conscious way, and sometimes the pain caused is entirely unintended. Before we worry about whether the other person meant to hurt us or not, it's important to recognise that something in us has been triggered, and to spend some time wondering about what happened and what we might want to do next.

To take an example from my own life, for a long time I struggled with a mixture of fear and anger when I encountered a particular volunteer. I wasn't sure why these feelings arose when she was around, and what information they might be giving me. I eventually worked out that I was tuning in to this person's potential disapproval of me (she was a powerful character), and then modifying my behaviour so I would be less likely to upset them. This meant I'd avoided raising a couple of important issues with them for fear of them becoming angry with me. I'd had to sit with my disappointment in myself for my lack of courage and integrity.

Once I'd identified what was going on, I had options. I could have continued to behave in the same way but with the clarity that I was currently making a choice to avoid them as I didn't have the capacity to do otherwise. I could have shared my feelings of nervousness with this person, or got advice from a colleague, or I could have gone ahead and spoken to them about the issues that needed dealing with. Any of these options would have felt better than continuing to half-ignore the anger and fear as a way of avoiding facing my inadequacy.

When we feel triggered it's usually worth pausing for a while before we take any action. This gives us a better chance of working through anything from our own side that is clouding our objectivity. We might realise we're still holding a grudge from a year ago, and try to forgive the other person for this past act before we look at the current situation afresh. We might realise that our flatmate reminds us of our dad when they complain about our untidiness, and that we are really more angry at our dad than we are at him. This pause can also include letting any anger or fear 'cool' before we make our response. In my experience, if there is anger or a need to manipulate staining my communication, it's much more difficult to reach a positive result.

Sorting through these complicated dynamics can take patience. We give ourselves as much empathy as we can, like putting an arm around the part of ourselves that is hurt or angry and asking it to tell us more. We ask ourselves which parts of the interaction we can take responsibility for, and when we can do something about what happened from our own end without having to involve the other person. This might be forgiving ourselves for saying 'yes' and promising ourselves that we'll say no next time, or realising that we were provoked into responding with impatience and apologising for our impatience. If we can be meticulous about owning our own foolishness, even if our foolishness was practically forced out of us by the other's behaviour, then it will be much easier to forgive ourselves, forgive them, and move on without looking back.

It is never okay for other people to abuse us physically, emotionally or sexually, regardless of our own behaviour. If this is happening, it isn't helpful to go through this process of sifting through and making sense, at least until after a firm boundary has been set. Regardless of whether we might have been involved in inviting the abuse in some way or not, we should say a very clear 'no' if we can and then do whatever we need to do to become safe. Leave the room for a while, leave the house, go to a friend's house or involve the authorities, and do whatever you need to do to protect yourself or your children. This boundary-setting is compassionate both towards yourself and towards the potential perpetrator as, regardless of what they might think at the time, acting out is never a satisfactory way of dealing with fear. We are protecting ourselves from being a victim of abuse, and we are also protecting the other from having the practise of being the abuser, which may well lead to further acting out and to others being hurt.

Deciding on what feels okay or not okay for us is a lifetime's art. Working out how to best 'steward' our body and our mental and emotional states in a world that is always making demands of us can take some practice. There are no guide-books, as skilful stewardship will look different for different people and will change over time. When a member of our congregation calls me out of the blue and asks if I can give them some advice, how I respond will depend on all sorts of factors including my past relationship with this person, the extent of their emergency, what my resources are in that particular moment, and how brave I am feeling about saying no! It's helpful to acknowledge that it's impossible to know what 'getting it right' is, and that we will continue to struggle with our human limitations. Good stewardship isn't about 'fixing' ourselves or others, but rather about learning to negotiate the stormy seas with a little more grace.

Telling people about our boundaries also takes some practice. I find that it is helpful to be clear and honest, and to offer alternatives – 'I would like to be able to listen to you talk about your problem but I am tired and I want to give you proper attention. Could we book an appointment for tomorrow?' This is also where Nonviolent Communication comes into its own – do have a look at the book by Marshall Rosenberg. If setting boundaries is new to you then you may do so unskilfully to begin with – there is usually a steep learning curve when we are learning new behaviours. You may also find that people will have strong reactions to your new boundaries, especially to start with – they will want things to go back to how they were before. Persevere! In the long run, those around you will thank you for no longer agreeing to things you don't really want to, and the inevitable resentment that will follow.

If we were Buddhas, we would have no need for boundaries. We would give whatever we could to whoever needed it, and we would feel no fear about running out or about becoming tired. If we gave all our food away and were left hungry, fine – we'd be hungry. As human beings, however, I think it is helpful for us to be realistic about our limits – to identify when we have been hurt so we can allow ourselves time to heal, and to let others know when they are asking for something that is currently beyond our capacity. We can aspire to become more helpful to other people, but they are not our responsibility. The Buddha will look after them. We only need to work out what our small part is, and to do that small part as well as we can. The rest will look after itself. We are trying to be good stewards, and sometimes we will get it wrong. Just like everyone else.

Questions for reflection

Do you have a clear understanding of what boundaries are? If not, how could you find out more?

How good are you at setting boundaries for yourself?

When do you struggle to set boundaries?

Who do you particularly struggle to set boundaries with? Do you know why?

How well do you know yourself? When feelings come up, do you take time to explore what might be happening?

Do you feel you deserve to say no or protect yourself from disrespectful or abusive treatment from others?

Are you putting up with anything you shouldn't be putting up with?

What are you most afraid of when it comes to setting boundaries with others?

Do you feel entirely responsible for someone else's well-being? Even if you do have certain responsibilities towards this person (e.g. if they're your child), can you see where your responsibility ends and theirs begins?

What boundary would you like to set today?

No blame

> *Sincere forgiveness isn't colored with expectations that the other person apologize or change. Don't worry whether or not they finally understand you. Love them and release them. Life feeds back truth to people in its own way and time.*
> *~ James Thurber*

My dear friend Terrance Keenan, a Buddhist teacher, has a motto which he uses daily – a six word set of instructions for life. "No blame, be kind, love everything." I have taken these words into my own heart and they guide me in all situations. If you're going to take any six words with you from this book, take these, and offer your thanks to Terry.

Each phrase is radical in its own way, and carries its own particular challenges. We'll begin with 'no blame'. Not a little tiny bit of blame, you'll notice – none. If you watch yourself over the next hour, you'll discover how often you reach for blame as a balm. I've just finished an argument with my husband, and I found myself throwing great clods of blame at him, recovering my equilibrium, and then tipping over into another round. I was only feeling overworked and overwhelmed because he did this and this and this, and if he only did that and that then I'd be fine. I can also blame the person who emailed me in crisis last night for the fact that I haven't done as much writing as I wanted to this morning. I don't want to take responsibility for my current state of overwhelm, or to acknowledge that I didn't have to send a reply to them until after I'd finished my writing.

There is a Zen/Taoist anecdote based on the teachings of Chuang Tzu about a man who's out one day in his little wooden boat on a lake. It's the boat's first outing after he spent some time lovingly restoring it. He's listening to the gentle splashing of water against the bow and enjoying the peace when another boat emerges from the mist. It seems to be moving towards him, fast. The man shouts – 'watch out!' but the boat keeps coming and smashes into the side of his, causing considerable damage. Anger rises up in him and he starts shouting – "What are you doing, you idiot? Didn't you hear me warning you? Look at the damage you've done!" As his eyes focus in, he realises that the other boat is empty. It had been carried on the currents and had no intention of causing him any damage. His anger leaves him like water through a colander.

This story reminds us that we are all empty boats, crashing into each other every so often and causing unintentional damage. My husband didn't do anything to deserve my blame this morning. He was simply the person in front of me as I came into contact with the 'damage' of feeling upset with myself for accepting too much work. A couple of the complaints I made about him did prick him, as I skilfully chose things which I knew would affect him, but if I'd really wanted to share how I felt about these things or influence him I'd have had a much better chance if I'd raised them at a different time. When we are complaining as a way of trying to feel better about ourselves, it doesn't dispose the other person towards open-hearted listening.

People often worry that a 'no blame' approach is equivalent to taking responsibility for everything that happens, including the things we're not in control of. Other people do behave unskilfully towards us, and sometimes they do hurt us on purpose, as a way of propping their egos up. We also find ourselves in situations like being made redundant or falling ill that we have little or no influence over. 'No blame' doesn't mean that we passively accept whatever happens to us, or that we take responsibility for the actions of others. Sometimes it is important to set boundaries, to hold other people accountable for their actions, or to speak up about things that are unjust. If our desperate debt-ridden niece has stolen some money from us, we make sure that we keep our money safe when she's around us in the future. We then take responsibility for our response to what they've done – giving ourselves what we need to slowly heal and, eventually, to understand and forgive them.

When people are hurtful to you or to someone else, it might help to remember that they are lashing out because they are scared. They might not know that they're scared, and they probably have all kinds of other justifications for their actions. They might rewrite their behaviour as reasonable, or think that they're paying you back for the times you hurt them. In my experience, however, we only strike out at other people if we are afraid of becoming vulnerable in some way – of being abandoned, shamed, seeing our fallibilities or of losing our last shred of self-esteem.

As soon as we recognise that we're blaming someone for our feelings or for some circumstance we're in, we can release them and so also release ourselves. We don't need to worry about them not receiving their punishment or 'getting away with it'. It takes energy to stay in denial, and it isn't comfortable to live with the niggle that all isn't well. People who hurt others are not healthy, happy people. We can also trust that life will show them the consequences of their bad behaviour if and when they are able to see it. If they continue behaving unskilfully, the world will just keep on being a mirror. When you treat your friends badly, they will step back from you and you'll find yourself alone. When you borrow money and don't give it back, people won't lend you money again. This feedback from the world is always an opportunity, and it may lead them to taking responsibility for their actions and beginning to feel or express regret, and it may not. That's not our problem. They will be busy blaming you or the circumstances for their actions – let them. To acknowledge responsibility for your pain may be too much for them. Our egos keep themselves propped up by any means necessary.

If we examine our own lives closely enough we'll see that The Universe doesn't let us get away with anything – but it always gives us the choice between taking the high road or the low road. Think about a painful situation in your life. The person who will be most affected by which choices I make is: me. Do you regret anything that you did, even if you were provoked? Acknowledge this, apologise for it and let it go, forgiving yourself. Do you need to set some different boundaries? Do you need to apologise to yourself for not taking proper care of yourself? Do you need recovery time? What have you learnt about yourself?

'No blame' means that we hand the other person over to the process of their inexorably unfolding karma, and we take care of the only business we can ever take care of – our own. If we practice 'no blame' in a radical way, we become radically responsible for ourselves. We discover that, even when we feel we have no choice, we are making a choice. Rather than blaming the system for forcing us to work so that we can support our family, we reframe this as making a choice to swap our time for both necessities and luxuries for our children. Rather than blaming our ex-husband for our current misery, we take responsibility for staying with him for too long. We can be compassionate with ourselves as we do this, seeing maybe that our parents never modelled how a healthy relationship works, but we still see the choices we made and know that we could have made different ones, however impossible this may have felt at the time.

Embodying this radical taking of responsibility is extremely difficult. Like all vows, we can point ourselves in the general direction of 'no blame', knowing that we'll fail often and sometimes spectacularly. When we are hurting, angry or afraid, we will do whatever we can to feel better about ourselves. We may cling more tightly to some of our blame stories than we do to life itself.

We all get scared – of being hurt, of losing something, and of not having enough. We handle this by hurting others, and by blaming others for our hurt. The only cure for fear is shining love on it. Sometimes this can take centuries, or much longer. But it always works in the end. Let yourself feel what you need to feel. Set boundaries or make amends when necessary or possible. Then release yourself from blaming.

Shine love on whoever has hurt you, and forgive them. Shine love on yourself and forgive yourself. Rest in delicious serenity.

> *God grant me the serenity*
> *To accept the things I cannot change*
> *Courage to change the things I can*
> *And the wisdom to know the difference.*

Questions for reflection

What objections arise in you when you consider the phrase 'no blame'?

How might these objections be keeping you safe?

When do you blame others or the world?

What are the results of this blaming?

What is your favourite story about how something is someone else's fault? How do you feel about this 'someone else'?

How would it be to release yourself from this 'someone else' by forgiving them?

How would it be to forgive yourself?

Which parts of yourself or others most need love shining on them? Can you start that now?

Be kind

Suddenly I understood that we must take care of things just because they exist. ~ Maura O'Halloran

The best kindnesses are those that are performed without thinking. Almost without knowing what he's doing, a man reaches out his hand in the night and moves a pillow to make his wife more comfortable. A toddler offers to share her sandwich with a stranger. A dog comes to rest his chin on his owner's knee. These kindnesses involve no calculation and no effort and they leave no trace – it is almost as if they are streaming through us, and we are the vessel.

All sorts of things obstruct this natural flow. One of these is a fear of scarcity. Wherever our heart is closed, we will cling tightly to 'mine'. 'Mine' blocks our impulses to offer to others. One way of unblocking our hearts is to intentionally practice being kind. We can notice when we are thinking unkind thoughts, and practice 'no blame' and empathy towards ourselves and the other until we feel a little warmer. We can also notice when we've become preoccupied with our own well-being and, after wondering if we're feeling afraid, look outside ourselves to see who or what might appreciate a little attention from us. We can 'fake it to make it' by doing something kind whether we feel like doing it or not.

Another thing that gets in the way is that we don't always have the resources to be kind. We may be low on energy after a period of growth or grieving, or we may just be out of kindness gas. The instruction to be kind also includes being kind to ourselves. Sometimes the kindest thing is to say 'not today' to our struggling friend and then to go and hide under the duvet for a while. Putting ourselves at the very bottom of the priority list can lead to a permanently low level of kindness gas, and this isn't a good thing to model to others. Extreme self-care is sometimes both necessary and helpful.

How can we practice kindness? Once we have begun to identify and remove any blocks, you might find that kindness begins to flow out of you naturally. It might also help to practice empathy. When we tune in to how it might be to be someone else we get glimpses of how people suffer, and we see their courage, their dilemmas and their own kindness. We can imagine how it might be if we were in their shoes. When we see these things we naturally find ourselves wanting to offer them something.

Giving things away is also a good way to practice kindness. I made a rule with myself a few years ago – whenever the thought arises to give something away to someone, I should do it. The thought came to me last week: "Give that book to Jenny," and so I did. Admittedly, I have hiccups, like holding onto the big bar of chocolate I thought I could give to Dayamay because I wanted to eat it myself. When this happens we can be kind to ourselves, notice our fear, and maybe buy another bar of chocolate to give to Dayamay...

A rather lovely side effect of being kind to others and to the world is that it makes us happy. When we are feeling sad or out of sorts, it can help to do something small for someone else. You could send a postcard to your friend's daughter, put a few coins into a charity box, stroke your cat's chin, re-pot the pot-bound houseplant, or just spend five minutes sitting quietly and sending warm vibes to someone who especially needs them. Being kind connects us to others and to the world, and creates a little gap in our carapaces where kindness can sneak in as well as out.

Etty Hillesum said that "We should be willing to act as a balm for all wounds." It is a beautiful phrase, and a little overwhelming. It is easier to be kind when we feel well-fed and rested, and when we feel warmly fond of people and the planet. Sometimes we are like empty skins, and sometimes people make it very challenging to be fond of them! That's okay. We notice this when it happens, and we do our best. We allow ourselves to be supported by the Universe, and we remember our self-care and boundaries, like plugging ourselves in to charge back up. We trust that we won't be asked by our Higher Power to give more than we have. We see that kindness is all around us, and we breathe it in and out.

Questions for reflection

When can you last remember receiving kindness?

When were you last kind towards someone else?

What might be blocking the flow of kindness in you?

How kind are you to yourself? What kind things do you do for yourself? What unkind things do you do?

How good are you at saying no? Setting boundaries? Self-care?

When do you block or resist your kind impulses?

What object would you like to give away to someone who would appreciate it?

Who needs your kindness right now?

What kind thing can you do for yourself today?

Love everything

You don't get to vote on what is. Have you noticed?
~ Byron Katie

I just had to unbutton my jeans. I thought they fitted well the last time I wore them, but over the past weeks I've been doing lots of writing and lots of snacking, and it could be that I've accumulated a little fat alongside the word count. I don't love the folds of flesh I see when I look down, not just because it's not 'the way women ought to look', but because it represents my over-eating as a substitute for being able to look after myself in healthier ways.

I didn't really want to start this chapter with a description of my stomach. But, as Byron Katie notes, we don't get to vote on what is. This is where the 'love everything' chapter begins, and so I'd better make the most of it. Let me try and follow Terry's advice...

What is there to love about my flabby stomach? Well, I guess I can appreciate that my body is doing what it should be doing – thoughtfully storing up fat for me and saving it for a rainy day. I can appreciate that I have plenty of food to eat when I want to eat. I can feel fond of my belly button, which once connected me to the person who grew me. That's pretty amazing. The skin feels smooth, and it's doing a good job too – holding in the stew of my insides.

Can I love the part of me that is greedy? That is more difficult. When I try, I veer away from the neediness in me, from the desperation. I persevere. Why might someone be feeling desperate? Because they are struggling with something, I guess. What am I struggling with? Some kind of panic? A hollowness? I can't get any closer than that for now, but I can at least feel softer towards the hungry-for-something Satya that shoves chocolate in her mouth.

As I type this, I notice myself taking a long breath and exhaling slowly. When we are afraid we hold our love back from parts of ourselves and from parts of the world – and yet when we do this, the love bends in on itself and starts to stink like over-ripe fruit. Sometimes we are in control of whether we can radiate our love into new places, like the process I've just taken myself through, and sometimes we're not. Sometimes the fear is too deep, like a dark reservoir that goes down almost forever, and the love stays put like a donkey who's planted her hooves and refused to budge. No point in dragging it.

Instead, we can use these two words like we use headlights. They will show us where we need to go. When they point in a direction that feels like an infinite cave of darkness, we can just pull over the car and keep pointing the headlights towards the cave. Notice the rocks on the ground that the light reaches – pick them up, become familiar with them, and put them down again when the darkness presses in too hard. Maybe bring a friend with you in the car. Remember that, even though you can't see what's at the back of the cave, there is always a Buddha in every hell realm, a bright spot of light that you can turn towards for consolation. Take breaks, and drive to the movies or to a garden centre for a while instead.

'Love everything' encompasses 'no blame' and 'be kind'. If we can truly love everything, the other two will come naturally – we will be able to forgive the terrible sins of others and of ourselves, and our kindness will flow from love. Write these two words down on a piece of paper and take it with you wherever you go – you will still be learning in twenty years, in a hundred years, in a thousand years. It is an advanced practice. It is asking us to become enlightened – to let go of every last scrap of our flimsy self-protection and to welcome everything in. As Zen master Dogen said, when we 'forget the self' and make our mirror dark, this is 'confirmed by the myriad Dharmas' as everything offers itself to us as-it-is. Violets, melancholy, this morning's cat puke, the shiny red garden chair, this empty mug, the blowsy roses that are blooming right now. When you burrow your nose into their soft honeyed scent you can't stop from exclaiming: Oh! Oh! Everything is vivid, abundant, heart-breaking, awesome, full of light.

Questions for reflection

What do you love?

What is more difficult for you to love in yourself?

What is more difficult for you to love in others?

What is more difficult for you to love in the world?

What might happen if you did shine love on these things?

When does your love refuse to come out? What might it be afraid of?

Which is most difficult for you, not blaming, being kind, or loving everything?

How might you carry these six words with you into your life?

Remember death

> *Why do you worry so,*
> *when none of us is spared?*
> *~ Jill Bialosky, from the poem 'Another Loss to*
> *Stop For'*

This morning I heard the news that our sangha member, Ed, died at midnight last night. He'd travelled with our Buddhist group from the earlier days of his kidney cancer diagnosis to his final weekend when we talked about the reassuring presence he'd experienced in his hospital room. He told me he felt he'd accomplished his final mission, which was making sure that his two young boys would be okay without him. Ed is gone, and now we will all go on without him.

We don't really talk much about death. I am lucky enough to have had a limited experience of it so far but, unless I die young like Ed, this is sure to change. Last year my therapist asked me whether I was engaged in preparing for death, and her question has stayed with me. I experimented with rolling the word around my mouth. Death. Death. It's actually a soft word, and as well as the anguish and the brutal violence of death I wondered if it was also possible to experience it as something soft – a blessing, or a gentle whisper in our ear. Don't wait to live your life. Don't wait.

I read a book by the undertaker Caitlin Doughty who, when she was a child, witnessed a girl falling from a higher floor in a shopping mall to her death. Amongst other things, the unprocessed trauma of this event sparked a need in her to get to know death more intimately. In the book she shares vivid details from her work in a crematorium – how orange mould bloomed on the cheeks of one woman, how coarse the embalming process is, and how they leave the babies to the end of the day as they burn so fast in the intense crematory heat.

As I spent time with Doughty in her workplace, I felt as if I was undergoing my own version of the charnel grounds meditation practice the Buddha prescribed for his monks. Charnel grounds are places where corpses are left above ground to decompose, like open-air crematoria. They were common throughout Ancient and Medieval India, and they can still be found in India today. The monks were encouraged to go to these places and to spend time with the corpses, noticing the changes that took place over time. The sutra where this meditation is described is full of gory detail, taking the monks from the first blooms of decomposition through to the stripped and bleached bones that are left.

What benefits are there to paying close attention to death in this way? Coming into contact with our impermanence transforms the way we live our lives. It places the mundane details of our lives into a much broader perspective. If our bodies are going to slowly melt into the ground like wax, do we want to plough so much energy into our anxieties about whether they are seven pounds lighter or heavier? Do we want to keep clinging to the grudge against our brother, which prevents us from seeing our nephew? Do we want to work such long hours?

Knowing that we only have a limited amount of time left (who knows how much) also helps us to prioritise. What are the important things today, and what do we want to complete this year? If I only had five years left, what would I want to finish? What projects or relationships would I drop? Remembering death can also help us to get these things started. We're often held back from starting new projects by the fear of taking risks, of failure, of disappointing others or of stepping in a different direction to the rest of society. If we're going to die whether we do whatever-it-is or not, then we may as well try it...

Knowing that we are all living in the shadow of death can also connect us to the tender spots in other people. The writer Caitlin Moran says that: "Only when the majority of the people on this planet believe – absolutely – that they are dying, minute by minute, will we actually start behaving like fully sentient, rational and compassionate beings." If we can probe into the depths of our own feelings about impermanence, we can at least guess at how it might be for others, and at what prickly or hurtful defences they might have developed to keep their fears at bay.

Caitlin Doughty founded the Order of the Good Death, for those who are interested in taking death back from the sanitised, arms-length safety of the current death care industry. She offers people an opportunity to help wash the bodies of their loved ones, and encourages debate and openness about our modern avoidance of the realities of death. Her book is both courageous and tender – she doesn't flinch from the sometimes disturbing facts of dying, and she is always thinking about how we can help those who are left behind.

It's been a few days now since Ed died. As I go about my routine – sitting on the blue bench and looking into the distance, eating peanut butter on toast – I have been conscious that these are things that Ed doesn't get to do any more. He can't ask how his children are getting on at school, try different drugs for his cancer, or attend another Buddhist service with us on a Wednesday night. His time on the earth is over. It is almost impossible to believe – as impossible as grasping the fact of my own mortality.

I am grateful to Ed for what he showed me about dying. I find myself less afraid of stepping into the Unknown Afterwards. If we are lucky, we will have a chance to engage in the process of our own dying as Ed did, and an opportunity to say the final things we want to say and to do the final things we want to do. We might not. None of us knows when, how or where our own death will come to meet us. If we are wise, we will try and live our lives in a way that leaves us prepared for death at any time. Tell your children you love them at the end of every phone call, and don't put the important things off. Appreciate the gift of each smile received, each life-giving meal, each shockingly pink sweet-pea, and every breath. Be grateful to your body while it is still working, and for the people around you who are still alive. Don't worry. Remember death. Lean into living.

Questions for reflection

How was it to read this chapter?

Who are the loved ones you have lost? Do they still accompany you?

Have you been affected by the death of your pets, or of people you didn't directly know?

How has your grieving process progressed? Have you given yourself enough space to grieve?

How do you feel about your own death?

What is the most difficult thing about your own imagined death?

What is the most difficult thing when you imagine others dying?

What beliefs, hopes or intuitions do you have about what happens to us when we die?

Do you find any solace in the idea of death?

What are the smaller deaths that accompany you – the death of parts of yourself, of jobs, of dreams, of friendships?

If you could focus on the fact that you are going to die, how might you change your life?

How can you begin those changes today?

Feel your feelings

> *People have a need to feel their pain. Very often pain is the beginning of a great deal of awareness. As an energy center it awakens consciousness.*
> ~ Arnold Mindell

We all try to avoid feeling our feelings sometimes. Feelings can hurt. Even getting in touch with our positive feelings can leave us afraid of our dependence, and of what we might lose. Feelings leave us vulnerable, as we lie like beetles on our backs with our soft bellies exposed.

We use all kinds of cunning devices to avoid feeling our feelings. One of our favourites is choosing from our menu of compulsions. I tend towards workaholism – filling my diary with things-to-do and moving quickly from one task to the next. I have complained for decades about having too much to do, and about not having enough leisure time. I purge my diary, leaving delicious-looking blank spaces, and then find myself filling them straight back up again. And what happens when I do give myself leisure time? I have no idea what to do with it. I flip between making more work for myself, and slobbing out in a way that leaves me over-full and floppy. It's only in recent years that I've come to realise how challenging holidays are for me.

My workaholism keeps me from having to feel any of my feelings. When I have a day or two off I often begin to feel a rising sadness – a kind of dull loneliness. It isn't a pleasant feeling. And so I put the television on in the afternoon, or start answering emails, telling myself it's so I can relax more completely later in the day. 'Later in the day' never comes.

We all have our favourite ways of avoiding feelings. What are yours? We also tend to avoid particular feelings more than others, as these are the ones which we hate to feel or which we worry will lead us to lose control. I very rarely feel anger, and yet I know people who feel anger as their first response to all threats. Some people will avoid feeling jealousy, or confusion, or grief. If we imagine the complete range of feelings as a language, it's interesting to wonder about our own vocabulary - which of our feelings do we use skilfully? Which do we over-use? Which do we tend to repress?

If there is a feeling that you often notice (and maybe criticise) in others but rarely feel yourself, then you can be pretty sure that you are repressing it! We can also sometimes catch our repressed feelings out of the 'corner of our eye' – seeing hints in our behaviour that there might be more going on than the story we're telling ourselves. In my own case I very rarely feel anger, but I do catch myself putting other people down. This might be a clue that something they've done has angered me, but I haven't allowed myself to feel any anger and so rely on feeling superior to them instead.

Another way we avoid feeling our feelings is getting seduced by consumerism. Philip Saltier says: "Americans become unhappy and vicious because their preoccupation with amassing possessions obliterates their loneliness. This is why production in America seems to be on such an endless upward spiral: every time we buy something we deepen our emotional deprivation and hence our need to buy something." This quote demonstrates the Catch 22 of repressing feelings. When we deny the existence of a feeling, it starts making more of a fuss – banging at the bars of the cage and demanding to be heard. This feeling of agitation may propel us even more deeply into our avoidance habits. If we continue to ignore it we are building up trouble for ourselves.

When I have some time off and I am able to experience my loneliness or my sadness, something quite different happens. I feel an intensification of the feeling for a while – maybe I'll have a cry, or lose my temper (usually at my poor husband), or both. As the feeling begins to be known and felt, I may have some insight about what I'm upset about and I might not. Either way, it's like something is flowing through me, from my stomach into my throat, or from my body out into the world. It is as if the feelings are getting processed and metabolised, like food in my digestive tract. The feelings become more dynamic and fluid, changing shape – from confusion to jealousy, or from anger to grief. After some time I tend to feel lighter, cleansed, and ready to get on with my day. Fully felt feelings tend to hang around for much less time than unfelt ones which can linger for days (or many years).

Feeling our feelings also gives us valuable information about ourselves, others and the world. In the example I used earlier, sometimes I notice that I put people down because I'm repressing some anger towards them. If I spend some time investigating what's going on, I may realise that I'm upset with the other person for not replying to my texts, but I didn't mention it to them because I was worried about upsetting them. Alternatively I may realise that they're not doing anything wrong, but instead reminding me of a past wound that needs tending to.

If I don't access the feeling fully, I tend not to choose how I respond but instead do what comes automatically. This will probably be a repetition of behaviour that kept me safe in the past but is now outdated and unnecessary. I maybe won't mention the texts to my friend but I'll avoid them for a while, or I'll let some of my frustration at them leak out. As we get to know the complex landscape of our experience, we see all our feelings as messages. We might sometimes choose to ignore these messages, like anxiety about applying for a new job we don't feel competent enough to do despite rationally knowing otherwise, but it's always good to know they're there and to acknowledge them before we dismiss them. Feelings can keep us safe as well as acting as signposts.

If we're so skilled at avoiding them, often without even knowing that we're doing it, how do we entice our feelings out? I imagine my feelings and the feelings of others as trembling little mice. Even the big ugly feelings we repress are hiding from us because they are afraid of what might happen if they burst out. Will everyone reject us, or will we really hurt someone? These mice need to be reassured that it is safe to emerge. What makes it safe?

We create a safe space when we reassure our feelings that they're not going to be judged by ourselves or by others. We trust that we'll survive, by remembering how we've survived feeling our feelings in the past, or by remembering the example of others. We create a safe space when we speak to people we trust about what's happening or about how we're feeling. It also helps to listen to ourselves, with empathy. We often need to be patient to tempt the mice out – noticing it when it pokes its nose out of the hole and not pouncing on it and pulling at it by its tail.

What if we do feel overwhelmed by the strength of our feelings, or by the idea of inviting them out? What if we're afraid that if we start crying we'll never stop? It's okay to give ourselves permission to dip our toes into our feelings and step out again. You might want to set a timer for five minutes and allow yourself a boundaried period of time to cry or feel sad or angry. As the feelings arise, notice how they become physically present in your body. Develop the cool and accepting witness who watches what happens from a slight distance, and if you begin to feel overwhelmed, step back into the witness – 'oh, her breathing is speeding up'. 'Oh, now she's having thoughts about how unbearable it is.' This witness is not feeling the anxiety herself, she's just watching. You might have to step back again and again, and if you start judging, witness that as well: 'oh, she thinks she's not doing this witnessing very well'.

Learning to feel our feelings is a lifetime's task. If emotional intelligence was modelled for us when we were growing up we get a head start, but even if we are starting from a place of complete emotional illiteracy, we can still learn. I hope that as you learn to turn towards your feelings rather than slipping into avoidant behaviours, you'll get a taste of the benefits. You'll be more informed about your own process, and you'll have more choices. You'll find it easier to understand where other people are coming from, and you'll get how hard it can be to do the right thing. As well as the difficult feelings, you'll be more in touch with all the good feelings too – peace, energy, warmth towards your fellow human beings, joy.

Kaspa went away a couple of days ago, and I've been over-indulging in ice-cream and toast. I mentioned this to my friend, who suggested that I could wonder about what vulnerable feelings might be hiding behind the eating. I felt a very strong resistance to her advice – I wanted to be able to carry on gobbling toast, and I didn't want her to 'take that away from me'. If you take my toast away, how will I protect myself from whatever it is I'm trying to avoid? Maybe I'll do some writing in my journal this afternoon, and see what emerges. If nothing else, I'll tell the mice that I know they're back there hiding, and that I'll try to look after them as best I can. They feel better already.

Questions for reflection

How do you avoid feeling things?

What are your favourite feeling-avoiding compulsions?

What is the most difficult feeling for you to experience?

Which feelings do you dislike seeing in others? When can you identify feeling like this yourself?

What can you feel more easily? How does it affect you to feel it?

Which little mice noses have you caught site of recently? Sadness? Resentment? Fear?

How can you make a safer space for your feelings to venture out?

When is it difficult for you to understand what other people are feeling, or why they feel what they do? How does this relate to other feelings in yourself?

How can you bring more kindness to the whole process of listening for your feelings?

What do you feel right now?

Relax

> *It often seems to me that the central function of therapy is to support the client in relaxing - as simple as that. When we can relax, the change that needs to happen occurs of its own accord. When we are in a state of tension, it doesn't matter how much we understand our stuckness - we still stay stuck.* ~ Nick Totton

I'm currently mid-way through my writing retreat in Shropshire. Before lunch I worked out how much of this book I had left to write, and divvied it up so I'd have the book finished before I leave in a few days time. As I get ready to resume work there is a big ball of pressure in my stomach. Get writing! Come on, hurry up!

In front of me the deep office walls bow to an upright-rectangle window. Under a strip of sky is a wooded hillside, a thousand shades of green, the homes of birds who are singing their hearts out. As I watch, a single dandelion seed parachutes in from god-knows-where and comes to rest on my desk. I look for the right words to show you these things, like choosing pebbles from a beach, and I notice my shoulders dropping and my stomach relaxing. I remember that it isn't about how quickly I rack up the words. Good writing is about selecting them precisely and arranging them carefully, as I rearrange this sentence and swap 'tot' for 'rack'. What matters is how much love I pour into these pages.

The opposite of relax is clench. Notice how the words feel different in your mouth; the claustrophobic tightness of 'clench', or the last syllable of 'relax' opening your jaw and encouraging it to soften. We clench our muscles when we are afraid. We often have good reasons to be afraid – maybe someone has threatened to hit us, or has taken something from us, or has cut us with their sharp words. Our muscles and our minds remember, and they clench again when something similar seems to be happening. They think that they are helping us by staying tensed, ready to get us out of there or to punch back. This tenseness lingers and sinks more deeply into our bodies and into our consciousness. It stays alert through the long nights, without our permission, siphoning off energy and blocking growth.

How do we relax? Sometimes it is as simple as taking a single, deep breath. As we let out the air with a deep sigh we can feel something shifting, something beginning to unfold. Sometimes relaxing is a longer process that begins when we notice where we are tense. Are we holding tension in our feet or in the muscles over our eye-brows? Do we tighten when we think about our new colleague, or a particular project? Are we clinging on to a hope for the future so tightly that the blood is draining from our fingers? As we continue to bring gentle attention to the tense parts, they begin to relax of their own accord. Our bodies and our minds want to relax, but they need to be reminded that they can. They need to know that they are off-duty now, and that we'll look after things.

How do we help others to relax? We listen to them and we hold them and we remind them of the benevolent Universe which is also holding them. We don't pretend that they will never be hurt again, because they will – but we tell them that we trust that they will handle getting hurt, and that they will get up again and keep on going. We offer them big squishy cushions and cups of tea. We give them plenty of time. We share our own messy lives with them and laugh fondly at ourselves, demonstrating how lovely it feels to be relaxed.

Everything looks different when we look at it through relaxed eyes. When we fall, we bounce rather than shatter. We bend in the wind rather than splitting. Whatever needs to move through us can begin to move through us, and we allow it through. Be like our bunny Poppet who keels over in the sun, for the bliss of exposing her long soft belly to the warmth.

Questions for reflection

What is happening in your body right now? Where are you tense? Where are you relaxed?

If you dwell for a while in the parts of your body that are relaxed, what happens?

If you dwell for a while in the parts of your body that are tense, what happens?

Be curious over the next twenty four hours – when do you notice yourself tensing up?

What helps you to relax? How could you do more of it?

Who helps you to relax? Which spaces help you to relax? Does your Higher Power help you to relax?

How do you help other people to relax?

How is this book helping you to relax?

Can you take a slow, deep breath right now?

Trust the process

> *If there is one thing I've learned in thirty years as a psychotherapist, it is this: If you can let your experience happen, it will release its knots and unfold, leading to a deeper, more grounded experience of yourself. No matter how painful or scary your feelings appear to be, your willingness to engage with them draws forth your essential strength, leading in a more life-positive direction.*
> ~ John Welwood

There are a lot of books, therapies, diets and philosophies out there which promise quick results. In my experience as an ordinary person and as a psychotherapist, deep change is glacially slow. This is painfully evident in my old diaries, where I read back five, ten or twenty years and recognise much more than I would like to. Back then I was writing about the same struggles I have now – overeating, overworking and internet addiction, and of how difficult it was to speak up in my relationships or to engage in self-care.

Despite these familiar themes, the Satya I read about is also a completely different person to the one I am now. Deep change has happened and I live a radically different life now. I have a religion which is the bedrock under my feet, I'm married to a wonderful man, and my friendships are much healthier. I took up yoga a few months ago, and it's the first time I've done daily exercise in my life. Before you get the wrong idea, there is still a teensy bit of room for improvement. I continue to grapple with my bad habits, and a couple of dormant ones sometimes make a reappearance. Still – deep change has undoubtedly occurred.

We would all like to evolve into improved versions of ourselves. We want to be just a little bit more patient, we want to do a little bit more exercise or eat a bit more healthily, we'd like to be a bit more disciplined... Why is this kind of change so slow? The foundations of our 'way of being in the world' were laid very solidly when we were small. When we were helpless eating-machines, depending on others for everything, the only thing we had any control over was the influence we had on our parents. We might not have been able to work our own limbs, but we could make a noise... To begin with we might learn that when we cry, we get food.

Later we might discover that when we cried too hard or for too long, our mother's face would close down and she would leave the room. When we are very small, a fear of abandonment is the same as a fear of death. We are very motivated to learn the lessons of being skilful in relationships, and the lessons we learn will depend on the capacity of our fallible parents, and on the complex lessons they learnt from their own parents. The next time we notice our mother's face changing, we might choose to stifle our cries. Our mother stays, and we have scored a victory. Thirty years later we find that we're still hiding our angry or sad feelings from our husband, as we're unconsciously afraid that if he sees them he'll leave us just like our mother did.

The strategies we develop for influencing others and for keeping ourselves safe become more complex over time, and sometimes they take on a life of their own. Maybe we started flirting with men as a way of getting power, and decades later we hate how this demeans us but we find ourselves unable to stop. Maybe we used reading to comfort us when we were a lonely teenager, but now we find ourselves wasting whole weeks hiding in novels. What do we do if we feel desperate to change but find ourselves utterly unable to do so?

If the behaviour we want to stop is causing anyone grave harm or is seriously threatening our well-being, we should seek help without delay, seeking professional advice or booking ourselves into a rehabilitation programme. If our behaviour is simple exasperating or demoralising, my suggestion instead is that we can learn to live gently alongside the parts of ourselves we wish were otherwise. We can appreciate that these dysfunctional parts are trying their best to keep us safe. Maybe we don't have enough alternative resources in place yet to let them go. The behaviours that we're so keen to get rid of were developed for a reason, and if we cut out and remove a defence mechanism before we're ready it might throw us into overwhelm. Continue to live a life of recovery – no blame, be kind, love everything – and trust that the change will happen when the time is ripe. This may not be on your schedule, but your Higher Power's schedule is always wiser than yours.

The good news is that when we're talking about shifts in our foundations, very small shifts can have all kinds of positive repercussions higher up. I imagine my day to day behaviour as the top of a tall Heath Robinson style tower which is supported by all sorts of deep beliefs, survival mechanisms and fears. I can spend lots of time rearranging the furniture on the upper levels, trying to eat more healthily or reading self-help books, and some of this work will have a limited effect. The massive shifts, though, like becoming Buddhist or falling in love with my husband, weren't in my control. I simply put myself in good conditions, had faith, and when the time was right a brick was removed or added, deep deep down. This had a profound effect on the whole Satya building, and led to all sorts of changes in my daily life, but these behaviour changes were a natural consequence of the bricks lower down, and I didn't have to work at them at all.

As well as trusting the speed at which processes unfold, I believe that we can also trust their direction. In our first session I tell my psychotherapy clients that the sessions will take us where we need to go, even if we're not sure where that is until much later on. If the client simply talks about whatever they feel moved to talk about, we will be led through a process of uncovering truths and making new choices. I also tell clients that the therapy will probably get difficult at some point, and that this is the point at which it's more important than ever to keep coming back. I have seen clients struggle with the 'dark before the dawn' many times, and also experienced this in my own life. I have faith that if we can stay with the process, especially when it begins to be uncomfortable or downright painful, we will be led forwards into the light.

The process of deep change is slow, mysterious, unpredictable, and mostly beyond our control. Understanding this releases us from the guilt of not trying harder or forcing change more quickly. We can admit that we don't know all the answers, and lean into negative capability. Negative capability is our capacity to rest in not-knowing without an 'irritable grasping after facts' (from Keats) – we can settle into a space of not-being-sure. This is notoriously difficult for security-loving humans, but if we manage it then we do feel better. The psychologist D. W. Winnicott said that "Acceptance of not-knowing produces tremendous relief."

Trusting the process involves leaning into something that knows better than we do, whether that's the process unfolding within a single human being, between a psychotherapist and their client, or between the nations of the world. As the process evolves, it may not carry us in the direction we want to be going. What I guarantee is that we can trust it – in time it will bear fruit, and they will be juicy and sweet.

Questions for reflection

What parts of yourself or your life would you most like to change?

What are the parts of yourself or your life that can seem impossible to change? How might these parts of yourself be protecting you?

When are you most impatient for change?

What processes are currently unfolding in your life? Are you making changes in your intimate relationships? Your friendships? Your work? Your habits? Your creative life?

Who might be the best people to accompany you as these processes unfold?

What feels difficult at the moment? How would it be to see this difficulty as a part of the unfolding process, and to trust that it will take you somewhere good?

Have you witnessed difficult processes unfolding in other people? What helped them? What was the end result?

What has helped you to trust the process in the past?

What might the fruits of your current processes be?

Open to the Other

> *Profound liberation is available to us when we allow our self-constructed narratives to dismantle and the world to then break in.* ~ Michael Stone

It is the beginning of the last day of my writing retreat, and I have a long day's writing ahead of me. I sat quietly for a few minutes before I began. I felt inadequate, insignificant, and definitely not up to the task ahead. Last night I was foolish enough to read some Annie Dillard and some Anthony de Mello, and decided that if I couldn't write as lyrically as Annie or as wisely as Anthony then I might as well pack it in. With these thoughts swirling in my head, I paused at the keyboard and listened.

Wood pigeons are cooing their throaty coo, and blackbirds and chaffinches are doodling on the treble clef. I thought for a moment about their singing. How was it to be that chaffinch? Was he worried about whether his song would compare favourably to the blackbirds? It didn't sound like it. It sounded like he was opening his throat and letting his music out. It was his music – nobody else's. I can't write a Dillard or a de Mello, and neither should I try to. My song is a Robyn's song, and only I can sing it. I am ready for my day of writing.

In this way, we let the Other break in. My self-constructed narrative is powerful. It has been fashioned from a lifetime of cushioning myself from the blows of the world – the disappointment of my parents, the teasing of my fellow schoolmates, the criticism of my colleagues. I had a good childhood – my parents loved me, and I was protected from much of the darkness of the world – but we are vulnerable creatures, and when we are wounded at a young age the scabs grow thickly and our defence mechanisms are fierce.

If we displease our parents when we are very small, we have no way of knowing that they won't leave us on a hill to wither away. Creating coherent explanations of how the world works and feeling acceptable enough to not be rejected literally become survival issues. As a result, the stories we build about ourselves and about the world are more stubborn than we can imagine. In order to maintain them, we weave all the new information we encounter into our old stories, ignoring those pieces that don't seem to fit. If my mother can't bear her children to feel jealousy, then I won't be a jealous person – even when I am presented with clear evidence to the contrary later in life.

The world is full of wisdom. It is gently knocking on our door without ceasing – listen to me! Look at me! I know something that you are excluding from your view of the world, because it threatens you. It holds the key to your next decision, your relationship problems, or your happiness. What a shame that the wisdom being offered looks like a vial of poison. We recoil from the things that threaten to heal us because we are afraid of being healed – we are afraid of becoming vulnerable again, afraid of feeling our feelings, and afraid of falling back in love with the world, with ourselves and with others. How safe we feel behind our scabs! How pale and thin our soft new skin is!

The poet Marie Howe speaks of this process in an interview: "...anything that pushes us into the depths of our being is very hard to bear. I find it hard to bear. Sometimes I open a book that's so beautiful I have to shut it because it hurts me. I can't stand it. It's like, Oh no! Oh no! Oh no! This is going to drive me into my own heart. A day or two days later I'm saying, All right, and I just surrender to it: Do it to me. Go ahead. I want it. I don't want it. I want it. I don't want it."

It doesn't always have to be so dramatic. We can begin to soften our self-constructed prisons in small ways. We can pause for five minutes before we begin writing, and listen to the wood pigeons. We can notice when we are clinging tightly to a story about ourselves or about the world, or strongly discounting someone or something, and wonder if there might be a different way of seeing it. We can write *small stones*. We can remember that the world doesn't want to hurt us (although sometimes we will be hurt). We can open ourselves to the gifts of grace – a kind gesture from a stranger, a revelatory dream, blackbirdsong. We can keep an open mind and expect to find wisdom outside ourselves wherever we go.

Questions for reflection

What is around you right now? Stop, look and listen. What wisdom is there?

When are you most likely to cling to your self-constructed narrative?

How do you feel about the Other – anything that is not-you?

Do you feel that the Other is able to help you?

When has the Other helped you in the past?

When have you felt wounded by the Other? Is there anything you'd like to say to it, or is there anything you can do to facilitate your healing?

How do you make sense of 'opening' to the Other?

Is there a particular problem you've been struggling with? How could you become open to gathering more information about the dilemma? Where might you look?

Do you have a particular question you'd like to ask the Other? Go out into nature, or find a quiet space, and ask it. Keep your ears, eyes, mouth, nose and fingers open. See what emerges.

Just as you are

> *You are flawed, you are stuck in old patterns, you become carried away with yourself. Indeed you are quite impossible in many ways. And still, you are beautiful beyond measure. For the core of what you are is fashioned out of love, that potent blend of openness, warmth, and clear, transparent presence.* ~ John Welwood

As I reach the end of this book I'm feeling as wobbly as a brand new foal. I really want these slogans to give you everything you need, but I'm sure I've left gaping holes. I know you'll see flaws in me that I can't yet see myself, and I want to go back and edit them out but I don't know how. I want you to like me. And then I hate that I want you to like me, which demeans us both, and which makes me wonder if I'm any less flawed than I was twenty years ago. Maybe I'm getting worse...

Sigh. As I get up to fetch another biscuit, I catch sight of my Medicine Buddha sitting on the window-sill. In one hand he's cupping a bowl of medicine and in the other, pinched between the tips of his thumb and index finger, he holds a sphere the size of a big marble. He looks at me serenely – taking it all in. He sees all the insecurities, all the attempts at manipulation, all the deluded pride and all the bitter failings. He sees it all and he loves me just the same.

We all slip into believing that we need to Do Good Stuff in order to validate our existence here on earth. We think we need to achieve snazzy things at work, help our neighbour, do sit-ups, earn more money, obey the self-improvement books, or even just do the washing up before we become a worthwhile person.

What I remember when I look at the Buddha is, without doing any of those things, I am already loveable. Not when I've finished this book and it becomes a surprise best-seller, but right now. Right in the middle of my messy struggle, with a trail of biscuit crumbs behind me.

What I would love for you to receive from this book is a glimpse of how it is to feel acceptable just as you are. It doesn't matter if you believe in a Higher Power like the Buddha or not – this feeling can come from anywhere that isn't you, including people and groups. It can come from me. I am beaming it out to you right now. Can you feel it?

> *just as you are –*
> *really*
> *just as you are*
> *~ Hisao Inagaki*

Questions for reflection

How does it feel to read the words 'just as you are'?

Have you ever felt accepted by someone who loved you? What was the feeling like?

Which are the parts of you that feel most unacceptable?

How might these parts look through the eyes of the Buddha?

Can you imagine that they might be the parts of you that need your love the most?

What helps you to feel acceptable just as you are?

When do you notice yourself doing things in order to be of value or so you'll be accepted by others?

Pause for a few minutes right now and rest in knowing that you are loved just as you are. Repeat as necessary.

Postscript

The morning after finishing this book, I awake to the unmistakeable sound of our cat Roshi vomiting. I get up and clear up the cat vomit for the umpteenth time this week, and print out my manuscript for a final check. I check the printed pages half-way through and discover that the printer has developed a stutter – it has printed the first eleven pages, stopped and then begun again from the beginning. Over and over again. There are reams of wasted paper. I spend the next hour trying to fool it, turning it off and on again or printing a few pages at a time, before admitting defeat and going upstairs to use my husband's printer. It is out of ink.

My guess is that your life will also consist of a good deal of mundanity and frustrations. How does clearing up cat vomit fit with some of the lofty ideas in this book: making vows, making space to create, loving everything?

We live in this world, and our job here includes clearing up cat vomit and disposing of pubic hairs in the guest bathroom. It is our privilege to clean up other people's messes, although it might rarely feel like it. We are doing our bit to tidy the world up and to make it beautiful. It helps to remind ourselves that we are making our own messes all the time. How many times did our parents change our nappy when we were babies? Look after us when we were poorly? How many times have our words stung other people? How many being's deaths have we been responsible for? How much waste do we produce with the food we eat and with the goods we buy?

After my anger at the printer cooled, I was able to smile at myself. Who am I to write this book? I am nobody: someone who gets tangled in the internet, who doesn't understand politics, and who loses her temper too easily. I also have some very important things to offer the world, and it is my duty to offer them.

You are the same.

An autumn night...
don't think your life
didn't matter.
~ Basho

The Right Medicine

If you're struggling with a particular problem, close your eyes and let your finger be guided to the appropriate slogan. Choose one or two, and carry them around with you for the next few days. See what light they might cast on the problem you have, or on your life more generally. Hand your problem over to the Universe to look after and let the answers come to you rather than seeking them out. If nothing emerges, try the exercise again in a week or two. Have patience. Go gently.

Begin here * Be bombu * Let the light in * Rest * Wake up * First things first * Listen to your body * Eat art * Do something small * Embrace dependency * Find fellow feeling * Surrender control * Grow gratitude * Hand it over * Structures support us * Make space to create * Everything changes * Hold on * Keep walking * Nature heals * Know yourself * Peaks and troughs * Detach with love * Bow often * Ask for help * Chuck should * Be heard * Change your conditions * Progress not perfection * Lean in * Attend to others * Seek sangha * Make offerings * Take refuge * Honour work * Make mistakes * Lighten up * Radical honesty * When you can't stop it, clock it * Let go of clinging * Savour solitude * Step towards fear * If in doubt, wait * Write things right * Make vows * Simplify * Find faith * Open your heart * Choose joy * Pray * Set boundaries * No blame * Be kind * Love everything * Remember death * Feel your feelings * Relax * Trust the process * Open to the Other * Just as you are

Books that might help

Here's an idiosyncratic list of books that have helped me beyond measure.

All David Brazier's books (also known as Dharmavidya) – start with 'The Feeling Buddha' or 'Who Loves Dies Well'.

'The Big Book' and all related 12 step literature (or even better, go to an open 12 step meeting). Russell Brand's book 'Recovery' is worth looking up.

Terrance Keenan's beautiful book 'Zen Encounters with Loneliness'.

The poetry of Mary Oliver.

Self-Therapy by Jay Earley (and books by Richard C Schwartz) that introduced me to Internal Family Systems, a wonderful way of getting to know the different parts of us and renegotiating the roles they all play.

Annie Dillard's 'Pilgrim at Tinker's Creek' and others (don't read her if you're in the middle of writing a book…)

The writing of Anne Lamott, especially 'Bird by Bird' if you're a writer.

'Sabbath: finding rest, renewal, and delight in our busy lives' by Wayne Muller.

A Little Book on the Human Shadow by Robert Bly.

Rumi, Hafiz, Kahil Gibran.

Carl Rogers' books on how to be a therapist and a good human being.

Neil Astley's wonderful trilogy of poetry anthologies: 'Being Alive', 'Being Human' and 'Staying Alive'.

If you're interested in Amida Shu Buddhism, 'Just As You Are: Buddhism for Foolish Beings' by Satya Robyn & Kaspalita Thompson. David Brazier's Questions in the Sand is also a great introduction.

'Timeless Simplicity' and other books by John Lane.

Mark Forster's books on time management especially 'Get Everything Done and Still Have Time To Play' and 'Do it Tomorrow and Other Secrets of Time Management'.

Pema Chodron's books.

'The Different Drum: Community-making and peace' by M. Scott Peck.

The fiction and poetry of Raymond Carver.

'Nonviolent Communication: A Language of Life' by Marshall B. Rosenberg, and other books on Nonviolent Communication such as 'What We Say Matters' by Judith and Ike Lasater.

'The Art of Asking' by Amanda Palmer.

'This Is How: Surviving What You Think You Can't' by Augusten Burroughs.